CHURCH MILITANT FIELD MANUAL

SPECIAL FORCES TRAINING FOR THE LIFE IN CHRIST

IMPRIMATUR: ✠ Robert C. Morlino, Bishop of Madison, 25 May 2012.

ISBN: 0615649920

ISBN-13: 978-0615649924

Deus Vult Press

3673 County Highway P

Cross Plains, WI 53528

For additional Search and Rescue Journal pages, Prayer Request Journal pages, and Church Militant Boot Camp Journal pages, visit the Knights of Divine Mercy website at www.knightsofdivinemercy.com

CHURCH MILITANT FIELD MANUAL

SPECIAL FORCES TRAINING FOR THE LIFE IN CHRIST

BY FR. RICHARD M. HEILMAN

✠✠✠

I am eternally grateful to God, my Father in heaven, and to Mary, who became so strongly my mother, especially after my birth mother, my best friend, June Heilman, passed to eternal life early in my priesthood ... a priesthood born out of her fervent prayers. But, I will never be fully capable of expressing enough gratitude for the gift of my birth father, my other best friend, Wally Heilman, who encouraged me to never settle for mediocrity, while he showed me how to put everyone else ahead of myself. Dad called it "respect." Dad's joy and resilience in the face of adversity came from never missing Mass and from one simple prayer: "Thy will be done." Thanks, Dad!

CONTENTS

INTRODUCTION:
THIS DAY WE FIGHT!

INTRODUCTION: THIS DAY WE FIGHT!

"We belong to the Church Militant; and she is militant because on earth the powers of darkness are ever restless to encompass her destruction."
— Venerable Pius XII 1953

0-1. In His Mighty Power!

This Field Manual is written to aid those of us in the trenches of the Church Militant to understand and train for our role in the mission of combatting evil and rescuing the souls of our loved ones who have lost the precious gift of faith.

Acknowledging this dire need, Pope Benedict XVI proclaimed the need for a "Year of Faith" that seeks to awaken humanity at a critical moment. "In vast areas of the earth faith risks being extinguished, like a flame that is no longer fed," the pope warned. "We are facing a profound crisis of faith, a loss of the religious sense that constitutes the greatest challenge to the Church today. The renewal of faith must therefore take priority in the commitment of the entire Church in our time."[1]

Pope Benedict XVI recently told the College of Cardinals that the members of the Church on earth are aptly described as "ecclesia militans," the Church Militant, since it is "necessary to enter into battle with evil."[2] In recent decades, we have seen Satan engage the world as never before. In all of human history we have never witnessed evil promoted so effectively while virtue and character and morals are roundly mocked and rejected. Meanwhile, it could be said that the Mystical Body — the Church — has never been so unprepared for and unengaged in the challenging mission of spiritual warfare. It is obvious that Satan's forces are well trained and well organized while ours are clearly not. At the very beginnings of our great nation, Sir Edmund Burke is said to have warned, "All that is necessary for the triumph of evil is that good men do nothing."

Here is a glimpse of the casualties of this lopsided spiritual warfare (these 2002 statistics have only accelerated in the past decade):

"In 1965, only one percent of U.S. parishes were without a priest. Today, there are 3,000 priestless parishes, 15 percent of all U.S. parishes. Between 1965 and 2002, the number of seminarians dropped from 49,000 to 4,700, a decline of over 90 percent. In 1965, there were 104,000 teaching nuns. Today, there are 8,200, a decline of 94 percent. A 1958 Gallup Poll reported that three in four Catholics attended church on Sundays. A recent study by the University of Notre Dame found that only one in four now attend. Only 10 percent of lay religious teachers now accept Church teaching on contraception. Fifty-three percent believe a Catholic can have an abortion and remain a good Catholic. Sixty-five percent believe that Catholics may divorce and remarry. Seventy-seven percent believe one can be a good Catholic without going to Mass on Sundays. By one *New York Times* poll, 70 percent of all Catholics in the age group 18 to 44 believe the Eucharist is merely a 'symbolic reminder' of Jesus." [3]

A society increasingly disengaged from the Divine Life has no place to go but down. Definitely not *progress*, but a radical descent away from our greatest potential.

> "For the past 50 years, every major institution has been captured by the radical secular left. The media, Hollywood, TV, universities, public schools, theater, the arts, literature — they relentlessly promote the false gods of sexual hedonism and radical individualism. Conservatives have ceded the culture to the enemy. Tens of millions of unborn babies have been slaughtered; illegitimacy rates have soared; divorce has skyrocketed; pornography is rampant; drug use has exploded; sexually transmitted diseases such as AIDS have killed millions; birth control is a way of life; sex outside of wedlock has become the norm; countless children have been permanently damaged — their innocence lost forever — because of the proliferation of broken homes; and sodomy and homosexuality are celebrated openly. America has become the new Babylon."[4]

Summoning us to courage, St. Augustine challenges us to fight: "Hope has two beautiful daughters: their names are anger and courage. Anger that things are the way they are. Courage to make them the way they ought to be."

As we said, the purpose of this Field Manual is to find the courageous faithful in the trenches of the Church Militant who seek the basic training that is vital for battling evil and rescuing souls. Yes, we are being called upon to fight the mother of all wars against powerful evil spirits in the heavenly realm, but we are sure to meet our demise unless we discover these battles cannot be won without first acquiring God's strength and mighty power:

> "Be strong in the Lord and in His mighty power. Put on the full armor of God, so that you can take your stand against the devil's schemes. For our struggle is not

against flesh and blood, but against the rulers, against the authorities, against the powers of this dark world, and against the spiritual forces of evil in the heavenly realms" (Eph 6:10-12).

St. Cyril of Jerusalem in his *Mystagogical Catechesis* insists, "Just as the Savior, after His Baptism and the coming of the Holy Spirit, went forth to vanquish the Enemy (in the wilderness), so you too, after Holy Baptism and Mystical Chrismation, having put on the whole armor of the Holy Spirit, are to resist the power of the Adversary and to vanquish him, saying, 'I can do all things in Christ Who strengthens me' (Phil 4:13)."[5]

"Let us be filled with confidence," St. John Chrysostom exhorts, "and let us discard everything so as to be able to meet this onslaught. Christ has equipped us with weapons more splendid than gold, more resistant than steel, weapons more fiery than any flame and lighter than the slightest breeze ... These are weapons of a totally new kind, for they have been forged for a previously unheard-of type of combat. I, who am a mere man, find myself called upon to deal blows to demons; I, who am clothed in flesh, find myself at war with incorporeal powers."[6]

0-2. Pope John Paul II's Master Plan

Pope Urban II launched the first crusade in 1095 with the primary goal of the Christian re-conquest of the sacred city of Jerusalem and the Holy Land. So great was the pope's speech in Clermont, France, on that day that the crowd was inspired to cry out: *"Deus Vult! Deus Vult!"* ("It is the will of God! It is the will of God!"). This became the battle cry of brave and noble knights who sought to recover that holy ground.

In our vastly secularized modern world, the need has never been greater to *reclaim the surrendered ground* of the sacred. While it was nearly a millennium ago that Pope Urban II challenged would-be warriors to "reclaim the sacred," in our day it was Pope John Paul II, in his January 6, 2000, Apostolic Letter, *Novo Millennio Ineunte*, who made his clarion call for us to put aside all fear and pursue daring apostolic goals which are rooted deeply in prayer. This is a call to return to our first priority, the universal call to holiness: "All the Christian faithful ... are called to the fullness of the Christian life and to the perfection of charity."[7]

The spiritual devastation of the last few decades compelled Pope John Paul II to draw up his master plan for the new millennium. In his plan, he emphasized the importance of "starting afresh from Christ": "No, we shall not be saved by a formula but by a Person." Thus, he called for pastoral initiatives that would focus on "Training in Holiness" and "Schools of Prayer." St. Francis of Assisi affirms this training in holiness as the fundamental starting point: "Sanctify yourself and you will sanctify society."

Pope John Paul II challenges us to consider, "since Baptism is a true entry into the holiness of God through incorporation into Christ and the indwelling of His Spirit, it would be a contradiction to settle for a life of mediocrity, marked by a minimalist ethic and a shallow religiosity. To ask catechumens: 'Do you wish to receive Baptism?' means at the same time to ask them: 'Do you wish to become holy?' It means to set before them the radical nature of the Sermon on the Mount: 'Be perfect as your heavenly Father is perfect' (Mt 5:48)."[8]

0-3. The Catholic Method

The strategy begins by employing what Fr. John Hardon calls the "Catholic method," which has three parts.

Everything in imitation of the Holy Trinity! Part one: Find the believing Catholics. Part two: Train them. Part three: Organize them.

Part One: Find believing Catholics. This is a Catholic soldier's FM (Field Manual). It is 100 percent Roman Catholic, as it highlights and celebrates many of our Church's 2,000-year-old treasury of beliefs, practices, pieties, and prayers as God's revealed plan for us. This continuity with our ancient faith tradition must remain unbroken.

Part Two: Train them. Fr. John Hardon said: "If the Church is sanctifying, if the Church can make saints — and nineteen centuries is a very good record — it means we do what the Church tells us to do to become holy. This means therefore that provided we are truly loyal to the Church, know her teaching, follow it, know her precepts, obey them, recognize her legitimate superiors and follow their directives even when the obedience or the following may be hard, we will become holy. Anyone then who turns his back on the Church or decides to walk apart from the Church or even claims to be following a higher spirituality but independent of the Church is walking in darkness."[9]

Part Three: Organize them. *The U.S. Army Combat Skills Handbook* begins, "Modern combat is chaotic, intense, and shockingly destructive ... however, even in this confusion and fear, remember that you are not alone. You are part of a well-trained team, backed by the most powerful combined arms force and the most modern technology in the world."[10] It is reassuring and motivating for soldiers to know they are joined together with such a large and powerful force united in their resolve to overcome evil with good.

Yet, most of us "modernized" Catholics do not realize we already belong to a company that is infinitely larger and more powerful than the greatest military force on the planet. We belong to the *Communio Sanctorum* — the Communion of Saints!

What is the Communion of Saints? It is the three states of the Church: The Church, the Mystical Body, exists on this earth and is called the *Church Militant (Ecclesia Militans)* because its members struggle against the world, the flesh, and the devil. The *Church Penitent (Ecclesia Penitens)* means the holy souls being purified in purgatory who long to be in heaven. The *Church Triumphant (Ecclesia Triumphans)* is the Church in heaven.

The Communion of Saints is the unity and cooperation of the members of the Church on earth, in purgatory, and in heaven sharing with one another the supernatural blessings they receive from the Holy Spirit. There is no force capable of defeating this Holy Alliance when it is banded together in one accord, and the devil knows it. It has been his primary strategic mode of operation to fragment this alliance in any way possible. This is why our primary objective will be to focus on the restoration of this Holy Alliance in our united effort to sabotage the tactics of the devil.

0-4. Recon

Any combat training and tactical planning begins with a process of intelligence collection, analysis, and dissemination. Recon (reconnaissance) is a military term used to determine the enemy force's disposition and intention, gathering information (or intelligence) about an enemy's composition and capabilities. Dr. Peter Kreeft wrote: "You cannot win a war if you are unwilling to admit we are even at war or you don't know who your enemy is or you don't know what strategy your enemy is using."[11]

We have all witnessed how the dry wind of the enemy's militant secular propaganda campaign has hardened the hearts of so many of our family members, friends, and neighbors. Spiritually speaking, many have crossed into the dry and lifeless valley of the dry bones prophesied in Ezekiel 37. Dead in their sins, with the rigor mortis of indifference hardening their hearts, they are without the breath of the Spirit, destined for eternal damnation, unless some campaign of search and rescue is launched.

So why has the devil been so effective? What is his strategy? To better understand the tactics of the devil, it is important to understand his names: "diabolos" means "he who places division or separation," and "daio," the root of "demon," means "to divide." These names identify the two great tactical campaigns the enemy has deployed, especially in recent decades: 1) Cut us off from our (supernatural) supply lines and 2) Divide and conquer.

Cut us off from our supply lines

The first major strategy from the father of lies is actually as old as the Garden of Eden itself. It is simply to convince us we do not need God (Gen 3:5-6), nor do we need His strength and His power (Eph 6:10).

In modern times, we have witnessed this in the effective campaign of militant secularists who have sought to de-mythologize our faith, a flat out rejection of the supernatural power of God. Once the devil has us convinced that we can challenge him under our own natural power, or simply deny that he even exists, he's cut us off from the only real power capable of defeating him: God's supernatural grace.

More and more common is the modern "secularized" version of religion that sees it reduced to a kind of psychotherapy for self-actualization. Some seminaries seem to focus on training therapeutic practitioners rather than theologians. In other words, instead of seeing Jesus as *God with us* — a real and ever-present source of supernatural love and grace — He is reduced to a historic figure we simply emulate as a model in our efforts at self-actualization.

Sadly, this secular version of religion has become so prevalent that most people's eyes begin to glaze over at the mere mention of God's supernatural grace as a necessary source of power in our lives. St. Peter warns us to be *fortes in fide*, strong in faith, because the devil prowls around like a lion, looking for someone to devour (1 Pt 5:8-9). Lions size up a herd to find the weakest and easiest target. Once we are detached from God and His supernatural grace, we are powerless to defend ourselves from the tactics of the devil.

Our ancestors and all of the saints knew all about this supernatural power and strength and that being in a *state of grace* was the armor of God that was to be treasured and protected at all cost. Sacred Scripture sees this Divine Life in God (state of grace) as the "hidden treasure" and the "pearl of great price" (Mt 13:44-46).

In his *Prayer of Surrender*, St. Ignatius of Loyola identifies this as the only meaningful treasure: "Take, O Lord, and receive my entire liberty, my memory, my understanding, and my whole will. All that I am and all that I possess You have given me: I surrender it all to You to be disposed of according to Your will. Give me only Your love and Your grace; with these I will be rich enough and will desire nothing more."

Divide and Conquer

The second modern tactic of the devil is actually the very ancient military strategy of "divide and conquer." This strategy is defined as one that separates a force that would be stronger if united. As we said, the devil is roaming around like a lion that sizes up the herd to find the easiest target. He is also watching to see who is separated from the herd. Large, coordinated forces are difficult to defeat. If the enemy can separate us into small units or individuals, he can more easily defeat each one.

In 1957, just two years before the call for the Second Vatican Council and the crisis of faith that followed, and just before the revolutionary decade of the 1960s, Sister Lucia (the primary seer at Fatima) said: "The devil is in the mood for engaging in a decisive battle against the Blessed Virgin, as he knows what it is that offends God the most, and in a short space of time will gain for him(self) the greatest number of souls. Thus the devil does everything to overcome the souls consecrated to God, because in this way *he will succeed in leaving the souls of the faithful abandoned by their leaders, thereby the more easily will he seize them*" (emphasis added).[12]

"*Strike the shepherd and the sheep scatter*" (Zec 13:7). There's no doubt that the devil has focused his assault on the religious leaders of our day. While these leaders may have had noble intentions of charity and pastoral sensitivity, the results have been devastating. Decades of lenient, non-confrontational leadership have left the faithful feeble and prone to be "conformed to the pattern of this world" (Rom 12:2). St. Augustine once said, "Charity is no substitute for justice withheld."

The unfortunate laxity of discipline has permitted confusion and strife where there should be clarity and harmony, an authentic unity based on the truth. As a result, the modern trend among those who believe and teach falsehoods that directly contradict the Church's teaching is to consider these pockets of dissent as merely "differing tribes" within the Catholic Church. In this deceptive tribal system, those who believe in and teach *all* that the Church teaches are then considered *extreme* among these tribes.

Right or wrong, religious leadership seemed to calculate that it was better to refrain from "charged issues" for fear of offending some or even losing members. However, St. Peter Canisius cautioned: "Better that only a few Catholics should be left, staunch and sincere in their religion, than that they should, remaining many, desire as it were to be in collusion with the Church's enemies and in conformity with the open foes of our faith."

Furthermore, we see that, for many reasons, one of which includes very poor catechesis in recent years, modern Catholics have all but completely forgotten the strongest force in all of God's creation for battling evil and rescuing souls: The *Communio Sanctorum* (Communion of Saints). This exchange of blessings has all but completely shut down.

Spiritually speaking, the devil is doing all that he can to catch us isolated and unarmed on the battlefield — no spiritual armor, no spiritual weapons, and no comrades in the heavenly realm to fight alongside of us. In other words, the reason evil is promoted so effectively today is because we're ignoring God's offer of supernatural strength and power and ignoring the mightiest of all allied forces: the Communion of Saints.

0-5. This Day We Fight!

C.S. Lewis wrote: "Enemy-occupied territory — that is what this world is. Christianity is the story of how the rightful king has landed, you might say landed in disguise, and is calling us all to take part in a great campaign of sabotage."[13] The Catechism of the Catholic Church reminds us: "This dramatic situation of 'the whole world, which is in the power of the evil one,' (1 Jn 5:19; cf. 1 Pt 5:8) makes man's life a battle: 'the whole of man's history has been the story of dour combat with the powers of evil, stretching, so our Lord tells us, from the very dawn of history until the last day. Finding himself in the midst of the battlefield, man has to struggle to do what is right, and it is at great cost to himself, and aided by God's grace, that he succeeds in achieving his own inner integrity' (*Gaudium et Spes*, 37:2)" (CCC 409).

Are you ready to do battle? In the movie, *Lord of the Rings: Return of the King*, Aragorn calls his men to *throw down the gauntlet* against the forces of evil. Let this call be ours:

> "My brothers! I see in your eyes the same fear that would take the heart of me! A day may come when the courage of men fails, when we forsake our friends and break all bonds of fellowship. But it is not this day. An hour of wolves and shattered shields when the age of Men comes crashing down! But it is not this day! This day we fight!"

PART ONE :
INDIVIDUAL READINESS

PART ONE:
INDIVIDUAL READINESS

1-1. Drive to Strive

I was a kid in the 1960s, or as we like to refer to it in Wisconsin: "The Lombardi Era." Inspired by Coach Vince Lombardi and the many titles his Green Bay Packers won for our state, I worked very hard in high school and became an all-state lineman. From there, I headed off to college, fully intending to work my way up to become a Green Bay Packer someday, until a neck injury ended my football career in the first year of college.

While I never spent one day in the military, I believe those early years on the gridiron sowed the first seeds of a warrior spirit that prepares well for battle, empowered to combat the forces of evil and fight for souls. I've come to believe that the desire to enter the fight is a desire to enter into a genuine training in holiness, pursuing the goal of becoming one of God's champions. St. Paul put it this way:

> "Do you not know that in a race all the runners run, but only one gets the prize? Run in such a way as to get the prize. Everyone who competes in the games goes into strict training. They do it to get a crown that will not last, but we do it to get a crown that will last forever.

Therefore I do not run like someone running aimlessly; I do not fight like a boxer beating the air. No, I strike a blow to my body and make it my slave so that after I have preached to others, I myself will not be disqualified for the prize" (1 Cor 9:24-27).

St. Paul talks about a strict training and a desire to run in such a way as to win. Vince Lombardi would've heard these words from St. Paul many times in his life, as he went to Mass every day. In fact, he admitted, "I derive my strength from daily Mass and Communion." As Coach Lombardi describes what it takes to be number one, see if you don't recognize a bit of St. Paul in his words:

> "And in truth, I've never known a man worth his salt who in the long run, deep down in his heart, didn't appreciate the grind, the discipline. There is something in good men that really yearns for discipline and the harsh reality of head to head combat. I don't say these things because I believe in the 'brute' nature of men or that men must be brutalized to be combative. I believe in God, and I believe in human decency. But I firmly believe that any man's finest hour — his greatest fulfillment to all he holds dear — is that moment when he has worked his heart out in a good cause and lies exhausted on the field of battle — victorious."[14]

In reflecting on his father's ability to bring the best out in a man, Vince Lombardi Jr. wrote in his book, *What It Takes to Be #1*, that this kind of hunger for excellence is hard to find today: "We live in a time when authority is questioned, gratification is instant, morals are relative, ethics are situational, and the truth is apparently what we decide it is. We lead lives of comfort and ease and, as a result, we've lost our hunger to lead and achieve. Today, fewer people are willing to make the sacrifices that are necessary to become a leader."[15]

Yes, in this namby-pamby, "everyone-gets-a-trophy" world in which we now live, we've lost the "drive to strive." And yet, this striving cuts to the very core of who we are. The Church Fathers of Vatican II stated, significantly, "All the faithful of Christ are invited to *strive* for the holiness and perfection of their own proper state. Indeed they have an obligation to so *strive*" (emphasis added).[16]

Sadly, far too many people have become conditioned to cower when they hear the words, "strive for perfection." In the coddled culture in which we live, the reflex response is, "I'll never be perfect." Yet, Coach Lombardi said, "Perfection is not attainable. But if we chase perfection, we can catch excellence."[17]

1-2. Superior Ideal

Among the ways we have just let Coach Vince Lombardi inspire us, I want to focus on the most important one: He went to Mass and received Communion every day of his life. Pope John Paul II said the Holy Eucharist "contains the Church's entire spiritual wealth: Christ Himself."[18]

Precisely during a time when our culture was becoming disconnected from their True Source, Vince Lombardi remained firmly and wholly connected to his. No matter what Lombardi dedicated himself to, he never abandoned his true self as a child of God and devoted disciple of Jesus Christ. More than anything, he understood the necessity of receiving God's Divine Life, as he brought himself, daily, to the altar of our Lord to receive Him — body, blood, soul, and divinity — as the real source of power in his life. This was where his energy, his very life came from. Archbishop Fulton J. Sheen once said, "As a man must be born before he can begin to lead his physical life, so he must be born to lead a Divine Life. That birth occurs in the Sacrament of Baptism. To survive, he must be nourished by Divine Life; that is done in the Sacrament of the Holy Eucharist."

Lombardi understood that all things converge in Christ — He is the way, the truth, and the life. Cardinal Timothy Dolan wrote: "To know Jesus, to hear Jesus, to love Jesus, to obey Jesus, to share His life in the deepest fiber of our being, and then to serve Him — this is our goal."[19] There is no other authentic way to strive for perfection. Lombardi recognized this as the *superior ideal* that must never be abandoned, but interwoven into all of our pursuits, whether it is as a businessman or parent or professor or coach.

1-3. Courage and Contradiction

I'm not on a quest for Vince Lombardi's canonization, but I do believe he was a deeply respected figure who lived profoundly by God at the exact time our culture was unraveling and when it was all too easy to abandon God (as it continues to be today). How easy it was (and is) for so many to follow the crowd through the wide gate (Mt 7:13) of the many fads and trends of immorality, self-gratification, and anti-authority in the 1960s and up to today. Lombardi is yet another reminder that the real heroes of every age are those brave souls who courageously accept the challenge of integrity by ignoring the trends of their times while remaining true to themselves, even if it means being a *signum cui contradicetur*, a sign of contradiction, in the world (Lk 2:34).

The word "courage" actually derives its meaning from a Latin root word "*cor*" which means "heart." It means we are never more courageous than when we "have the courage of our convictions," that is, when we live from the heart, remaining true to who we really are. Lombardi was courageous because he simply yielded to his *raison d'être*, his reason for existence. St. Catherine of Siena put it this way: "If you are what you should be, you will set the whole world ablaze!"

Who are we, then, and what is our reason for existence? Sometimes the message escapes us in its simplicity. Jesus said, "I give praise to You, Father, Lord of heaven and earth, for although You have hidden these things from the wise and the learned You have revealed them to the childlike" (Mt 11:25). The Baltimore Catechism states who we are quite plainly: "We were made to the image and likeness of God ... to know Him, to love Him, and to serve Him in this world, and to be happy with Him forever in heaven."[20] The spiritual master, Fr. Thomas Merton, wrote: "To say that I am made in the image of God is to say that love is the reason for my existence, for God is love. Love is my true identity. Selflessness is my true self. Love is my true character. Love is my name."[21]

1-4. Spiritual Heroism

It was on the gridiron in the 1960s that Coach Vince Lombardi, fully grounded in this superior ideal, compelled his men to strive for greatness, never settling for second best. At the very same time, the Church Fathers of the Second Vatican Council were calling upon all of us to engage a spiritual heroism — *the universal call to holiness* — not settling for a second- or third-rate spiritual life. The challenge is to move "ALL IN" for God and His plan for our life:

> "The Lord Jesus, the divine Teacher and Model of all perfection, preached holiness of life to each and every one of His disciples of every condition. He Himself stands as the author and consummator of this holiness of life: 'Be you perfect, even as your heavenly Father is

perfect' (Mt 5:48). Indeed He sent the Holy Spirit upon all men that He might move them inwardly to love God with their whole heart and their whole soul, with all their mind and with all their strength and that they might love each other as Christ loves them."[22]

St. Thomas Aquinas was once asked: "What should I do to reach sanctity?" He turned and simply said, "*Velle,*" that is, "Will it." Fr. Jordan Aumann commented in his *Spiritual Theology* that "St. Teresa of Avila considers it of decisive importance 'to have a great and very determined resolve not to stop until one reaches (sanctity),' without reckoning the difficulties along the way, the criticism of those around us, the lack of health, or the disdain of the world. Therefore, only resolute and energetic souls, with the help of divine grace, will scale the heights of perfection."[23]

The Gospels stories show how Jesus touched people in ways that made them question the direction of their lives. Some turned away because His challenge seemed to be too hard. But many others were so moved by His mission and ministry that they were compelled to search for a more perfect way of living and being. Where do you stand? Are you ready to put it all on the line? This means nothing less than to do what God is calling you, from the depths of your being, to do; to rouse yourself to action on behalf of the kingdom. Are you ready to say "yes" to the call to become His *champion*?

1-5. Semper Fi

Latin for "always faithful," *Semper Fidelis* (shortened to *Semper Fi*) became the Marine Corps motto in 1883. It guides Marines to remain faithful to the mission at hand, to each other, to the Corps, and to country, no matter what. Becoming a Marine is a transformation that cannot be undone, and *Semper Fi* reminds them of that. OORAH!!!

This kind of unwavering dedication is exactly what Jesus meant when He gave us the criterion for enlisting in His elite fighting force: "If any man would come after Me, let him deny himself and take up his cross daily and follow Me. For whoever would save his life will lose it; and whoever loses his life for My sake, he will save it. For what does it profit a man if he gains the whole world and loses or forfeits himself?" (Lk 9:23-25).

While sounding like a Marine Corps drill instructor, St. John Vianney expounds on this radical call to discipleship:

"There is no doubt about it: a person who loves pleasure, who seeks comfort, who flies from anything that might spell suffering, who is over-anxious, who complains, who blames, and who becomes impatient at the least little thing which does not go his way — a person like that is a Christian only in name; he is only a dishonor to his religion, for Jesus Christ has said so: 'Anyone who wishes to come after Me, let him deny himself and take up his cross every day of his life, and follow Me.'"[24]

1-6. Look Him in the Eye, Soldier!

If we claim that we have fellowship with Him, and yet we walk in darkness, then we are lying and not telling the truth (1 Jn 1:6). Origen, in his commentary on this passage, writes: "No one can grasp the meaning of the Gospel unless he has rested on the breast of Jesus and unless he has received from Him Mary, who becomes his mother also."[25] Here we are identifying the entryway (or opening) into the Divine Life of God and the way of sanctification: *It must be deeply personal!*

33

Entrance into the Divine Life actually parallels the first day (birthday) of our Savior's life in the world and the moment the newborn baby Jesus is laid in the arms of His mother, Mary. Imagine the scene ... their eyes locked and through the windows of their adoring eyes they peered into each other's soul. What occurred was a bond of love, a semper fi *transformation that could not be undone.*

Throughout all of salvation history we see such cries as "Let His face shine upon you" (Nm 6:25) and "Do not hide Your face from me" (Ps 27:9, 69:17, 102:3). This face-to-face, "look-me-in-the-eye" bonding is essential in understanding the necessity for making a *semper fi* connection with Christ. This kind of face-to-face encounter with God changes everything as it calls forth, quite literally, *a transformation that cannot be undone.* It marks a major shift away from a "face-in-the-crowd," "Christian in name only," "do-only-what's-minimally-required" empty religiosity, into a totally dedicated (*semper fi*) loyalty in love that remains faithful to God, to each other, and to the mission, no matter what.

Pope John Paul II said, "Real love is demanding. For it was Jesus — our Jesus Himself — Who said: 'You are My friends if you do what I command you' (Jn 15:14). Love demands effort and a personal commitment to the will of God. It means discipline and sacrifice, but it also means joy and human fulfillment."[26] Mother Teresa said of love: "Love to be real, it must cost — it must hurt — it must empty us of self."[27]

"We have a tendency to think only about self-protection, safety, and avoidance of trouble," says Fr. Robert Barron. "This tends to be our primary frame of reference. But God thinks relentlessly in terms of love, even when that love entails suffering. So, we ask ourselves, what is our final frame of reference? Is it, 'How do I avoid pain?' or is it, 'How do I love?' So, if I wake up every morning and my basic question is 'How am I going to avoid pain?' then I am going to live my life in a certain way — ultimately, a selfish way. But if when I wake up in the morning I say, 'How do I love today?' then I will live the life of a saint."[28]

1-7. One Thing

Pope Benedict XVI said, "The heart open to God, purified by contemplation of God, is stronger than guns and weapons of every kind ... the Evil One has power in this world, as we experience continually; he has power because our freedom continually lets itself be led away from God."[29] The motto of the Evil One is *"Non Serviam,"* "I will not serve." Our daily motto must stand in contrast to this; it must be identical to Mary's: *"Serviam!"* — "I will serve!"

This brings us to the key to Pope John Paul II's master plan for the new millennium as he asks us to set aside our disconnected busy-ness and to start fresh by *contemplating the face of Christ.* It is clear that the Holy Father was encouraging us to place our emphasis on reconnecting to the Divine Life of God, which is classically referred to as the *unum necessarium*, the one thing necessary.

The "one thing necessary" constitutes the essential foundation for the interior life and consists in hearing the word of God and living by it (I will serve!). It stems from the story of Martha and Mary (Lk 10:38-42), where we first see that, amazingly, the Second Person of the Holy Trinity was sitting right in their living room. Now, Martha remains busy with the good and noble protocol of hospitality while Mary sits at the feet of Jesus, her eyes locked on His holy face, peering into His soul, hanging on His every word. Mary is actually in adoration, soaking in everything our Lord wants to give her. I like to say that

35

she is "Mary-nating" — soaking in the gusher of God's graces. Mary had come to understand what St. Augustine said: "God loves each of us as if there were only one of us." Remarkable!

When Martha objects to Mary's lack of activity, Jesus tells Martha that she remains anxious and upset about many things while Mary has chosen the better portion, the "one thing necessary" (*unum necessarium*). Mary was the one who was making the guest truly feel welcomed while Martha remained detached, going through the motions of the demands of protocol. God is light and love and truth Who brings order and meaning and serenity to our lives. While we remain disconnected from our Source, we remain easily agitated and frustrated in our disordered and chaotic existence as we continue to walk in darkness.

A very significant modern example of this is seen in the Martha-like indifference to the presence of the Divine in so many of our present-day liturgies, compared to a more Mary-like contemplative way of worshiping. Contemplative awe and veneration has always been the distinctive way Catholics worshiped, until recent decades. The unintended consequence of the modern initiative to push for a more irreverent way of worshiping that is performance oriented and man-centered, lacking in a deep sense of the sacredness of God, has led to an epidemic of detachment from the Divine, facilitating the modern prevalence of spiritual sloth (indifference towards spiritual things). Like Martha, God is "right there in our midst," but we act as though He is not, or if He is, "What's the big deal?"

Pope Benedict XVI (then Cardinal Ratzinger) stated that any real effort at renewal in the Church must begin with a new liturgical movement:

"I am convinced that the crisis in the Church that we are experiencing today is to a large extent due to the disintegration of the liturgy, which at times has even come to be conceived of *etsi Deus non daretur* (as though God were not there): in that it is a matter of indifference whether or not God exists and whether or not He speaks to us and hears us. But when the community of faith, the world-wide unity of the Church and her history, and the mystery of the living Christ are no longer visible in the liturgy, where else, then, is the Church to become visible in her spiritual essence? Then the community is celebrating only itself, an activity that is utterly fruitless. And, because the ecclesial community cannot have its origin from itself but emerges as a unity only from the Lord, through faith, such circumstances will inexorably result in a disintegration into sectarian parties of all kinds — partisan opposition within a Church tearing herself apart. This is why we need a new Liturgical Movement, which will call to life the real heritage of the Second Vatican Council."[30]

1-8. From Superficial to Supernatural

And so we see that it is a face-to-face, intimately personal, "divine connection" that is fundamental in understanding Pope John Paul II's master plan. The Gospel story he sets as the foundation for this appeal is the "Call of the First Disciples" (Lk 5:1-11). This is the classic scene in which Jesus tells Peter to "Put out into deep water (*duc in altum*), and let down the nets for a catch." Peter's response is: "Master, we've worked hard all night and haven't caught anything. But because You say so, I will let down the nets." They proceed to catch the maximum amount of fish their nets can hold. Peter, filled with awe and wonder once he realizes he is in the presence of divinity, does not feel worthy to be called. But Jesus says, "Do not be afraid, from now on you will be fishers of men."

Why does the Holy Father choose this particular Gospel reading as the basis for his new millennium master plan? Because Peter's words — "We've worked hard all night and haven't caught anything" — could not speak any more directly to the modern tsunami-like wave of secularism rolling across our planet, as well as our endless parade of parish programs that are mostly done as though God were not there (*etsi Deus non daretur*).

In other words, the story of the great catch is meant to show that when we try to move only under our own natural power without God (*we've worked hard*), we will flounder in the chaos of darkness (*all night*) and come up empty (*caught nothing*) every time. Jesus asks us to get in sync with Him (*to obey Him*) and not be afraid to set aside our superficial (*man-powered*) tendencies, as we enter the depths of a supernatural (*God-powered*) life.

Fr. Robert Barron puts it this way:

"What is eternal life? What does it mean to be saved? What does it mean to get to heaven? It means to participate to the fullest degree possible in the very life of God. It means conformity to love. It means surrendering to the grace of God and then allowing that grace to invade every aspect of your life, so that grace flows through you and into the wider world. That's what it means to be saved. That's what it means to be in the embrace of God. To be living God's life."[31]

Here is Christ's summons to enter the Divine Life, a life that offers the deepest kind of purpose-filled joy:

"As the Father has loved Me, so have I loved you. Abide in My love. If you obey My commands, you will abide in My love, just as I have obeyed My Father's commands and abide in His love. I have told you this so that My joy may be in you and that your joy may be complete. My command is this: Love each other as I have loved you. Greater love has no one than this, that he lay down his life for his friends. You are My friends if you do what I command" (Jn 15:9-14).

Everything in the religious order — sacraments, teaching, Scripture, moral discipline, preaching, etc. — is meant to bring us to this deeper state of being, to this Divine Connection. Jesus calls it "abiding." The Latin for this is "*maneo*" which means "to remain" or "to stay" or "to endure" (or like the Marine Corps' *semper fi*). This Divine Connection, this conformity to love, this participation in the Divine Life of God is the very power of the Holy Spirit and is referred to as being in a *state of grace*.

While far too many modernized Catholics have all but completely ignored the necessity of the divinized life under the supernatural power of grace, our ancestors could not conceive of life without it. "Grace," wrote Thomas à Kempis, "is the mistress of truth, the light of the heart, the comforter of affliction, the banisher of sorrow, the expeller of fears, the matrix of devotion, the producer of tears. What am I without it but a piece of dry wood and an unprofitable stock, fit for nothing but to be cast away."[32]

1-9. God Strong

The U.S. Army ran a very effective "Army Strong" advertising campaign to recruit soldiers. The key message was: "There is strong, and then there is Army Strong." The commercial goes on to say, "It is a strength like none other. It is a physical strength. It is an emotional strength. It is strength of character. It is strength of purpose. The strength to do good today, and the strength to do well tomorrow. The strength to obey, and the strength to command. The strength to build, and the strength to tear down. The strength to get yourself over, and the strength to get over yourself."[33]

These are warrior assets necessary to overcome the enemy. However, recall that our struggle is not against flesh and blood combatants, but against the much stronger and craftier spiritual forces of evil in the heavenly realm (Eph 6:11). This means it is not enough for you to possess the power of a warrior. You must discover what it means to be supernaturally empowered by God. You are to become not just Army Strong, but *God Strong.* You must know what it means to be in a *state of grace.* St. Ignatius of Loyola said, "Few souls understand what God would accomplish in them if they were to abandon themselves unreservedly to Him and if they were to allow His grace to mold them accordingly."

Fr. John Hardon wrote: "St. Thomas Aquinas believed ... that man is more than a composite of body and soul, that his is nothing less than elevated to a supernatural order which participates, as far as a creature can, in the very nature of God. Accordingly, a person in the state of grace, or divine friendship, possesses certain enduring powers, the infused virtues and gifts, that raise him to an orbit of existence as far above nature as heaven is above earth, and that give him abilities of thought and operation that are literally born, 'not of the will of flesh nor of the will of man, but of God.'"[34]

Jesus told St. Faustina: "The graces of My mercy are drawn by means of one vessel only, and that is — trust. The more a soul trusts, the more it will receive. Souls that trust boundlessly are a great comfort to Me, because I pour all the treasures of My graces into them. I rejoice that they ask for much, because it is my desire to give them much, very much. On the other hand, I am sad when souls ask for little, when they narrow their hearts."[35]

This is amazing! Jesus is telling us that we can literally grow our spiritual hearts to be capable of more and more of His supernatural graces. Our spiritual heart is a vessel, Jesus tells us. It's like a "trust bucket" that we bring to the well of God's graces. The greater our trust, the larger is our bucket for receiving His amazing supernatural grace. What's stopping you from possessing a huge trust bucket filled with many graces?

1-10. War on the Supernatural

The unfortunate reality is that the modern campaign of militant secular indoctrination has been so severe that far fewer remain who believe or trust in God's supernatural power. As a result, the spiritual hearts of many are reduced to the size of a thimble, only capable of receiving a few meager drops, if any, from the wellspring of God's graces (Rev 22:1-2). In spiritual terms, this makes us puny and scrawny rather than strong and powerful mighty warriors ready to confront the powers of darkness in the heavenly realm. With so many modernized Christians ignoring the reality of grace, it is no wonder that evil is thriving in our day.

In speaking of the need for a New Evangelization, Pope Benedict XVI said, "the true problem of our times is the 'Crisis of God,' the absence of God, disguised by an empty religiosity"[36] ... a kind of lukewarm, going through the motions of one's faith, which ends up collapsing completely. The terrible consequence of this war on the supernatural is seen in the epidemic of spiritual sloth in our times — hearts deadened to the Divine Life of God.

Fr. Robert Barron draws attention to this very real epidemic in our times:

"A real concrete statistic around this is that 70 percent of the baptized faithful are staying away from Mass on a regular basis. And we're doing well in comparison with the European countries. Vatican II said the Mass is the source and summit of the Christian life ... everything leads to and flows from the Mass. The Eucharist is everything, and 70 percent could care less about it. Yes, there are many reasons around why some do not go to Mass, but I suspect that, for most, they are suffering from spiritual sloth; they could just care less."[37]

Aristotle said, "No one can long remain in sadness without any joy."[38] Depriving oneself of spiritual joy through neglect and sloth leaves one desperate to fill that void with inferior pleasures. Hence, it is no wonder why we see so many people frantically attempting to fill their lives with every kind of activity and distraction possible, desperately trying to avoid the gloom of emptiness. St. Augustine said, "You have made us for Yourself, Lord, and our hearts are restless until they rest in You."

1-11. O.I.L. for the Fire

How then are we to prepare our restless hearts to receive the power of the Holy Spirit? Recall Jesus' parable of the 10 virgins (Mt 25:1-12), five of whom were wise and five of whom were foolish. When the time came to meet the Bridegroom and go in to join the festivities, the foolish ones did not have enough oil for their lamps. They were forced to go get more oil while everyone else went in to "join the dance."

Why has study after study shown that people of religious conviction are the happiest? For those who have yielded to a deeply devoted (*semper fi*) love relationship with Jesus, there is a distinctive serenity and joy about them. There seems to be an extra spring in their step and twinkle in their eye. Far from the boredom and misery of sloth, they radiate a supernatural love, joy, peace, patience, kindness, goodness, generosity, and gentleness (Fruit of the Holy Spirit, Gal 5:22-23). They are attracted to spiritual things. They have a resolve to lighten the burdens of others. They have a sense of purpose and mission. They seem to have discovered the way to "join the dance" of life.

In the meantime, like the five foolish virgins, there are those who seem to be "on the outside looking in," wondering what it takes to be invited to "the dance of life."

Now, the Holy Spirit is often depicted as fire. Jesus said, "I have come to cast fire on the earth, and how I wish it were already kindled" (Lk 12:49). When Pentecost arrived, the Holy Spirit appeared as tongues of fire that came and rested on the disciples (Acts 2:3). We know fire needs fuel to ignite, whether it's kindling or, as in the parable of the 10 virgins, oil for a lamp. Spiritually speaking, the Holy Spirit will come to rest on those hearts that have provided the fuel for its fire.

So, what is the fuel we offer for the Holy Spirit's fire? The word "oil" provides a superb acronym to describe the necessary fuel for receiving the fire of the Holy Spirit: O.I.L. = **O**bedience **I**n **L**ove. Blessed Charles de Foucauld called obedience the "yardstick of love." It's a clear way we measure the fidelity and unselfishness of our hearts. Jesus said that His yoke is easy and His burden light (Mt 11:28-30) not because He would ask less of us, but because He knew that love renders suffering bearable and even joyful. St. Ignatius of Loyola said, "It is not hard to obey when we love the one whom we obey."

Remember, it was Mary's *fiat* (yes) that brought the Holy Spirit: "Behold the handmaid of the Lord. Be it done unto me according to Thy word" (Lk 1:38). Because Mary submitted, the Holy Spirit came upon her, and she was

43

filled with the life of God. Spiritually speaking, the same thing happens to us once we are ready to set aside our foolish pride and humbly offer our "yes" to God. And, just as Mary delivered a Savior into the world, we are called to bring this Divine Life we've received to all we encounter.

Obedience In Love (O.I.L.) is what Sacred Scripture refers to as "fear of the Lord" or holy fear. As distinct from servile fear (fear of punishment), holy fear is a fear of disappointing or being separated from the one you love. St. Francis de Sales wrote, "We must fear God out of love, not love Him out of fear." It is like a son who loves his dad very much and fears disappointing him or damaging the relationship or being separated in any way. St. Paul wrote: "So you have not received a spirit that makes you fearful slaves. Instead, you received God's Spirit when He adopted you as His own children. Now we call Him, 'Abba, Father'" (Rom 8:15).

Why did the Bridegroom say, "I do not know you" (Mt 25:12) to the foolish virgins who did not bother to bring enough oil? They represent those who are stuck in that kind of empty religiosity that avoids the extra effort, the sacrifice that is vital in any real love relationship. Instead, they neglect, take shortcuts, or avoid altogether the greater demands of obedient love. Trapped in spiritual sloth (indifference), there is no holy fear and therefore, they are content to keep God at an impersonal, manageable distance as they remain just a face in the crowd — a pew potato — a bench warmer who is content to be on the team but avoids the effort of getting in the game. "Faith means battles;" said St. Ambrose, "if there are no contests, it is because there are none who desire to contend."

1-12. Free to Enlist in God's Mission

What is it that can snatch the Divine Life from us, killing off any zeal for God's mission of battling evil and saving souls? There are actually three wounds that ravage souls and bring spiritual death to them by turning away from God. St. John speaks of these evils when he says: "For all that is in the world — the lust of the flesh (craving for sensual gratification) and the lust of the eyes (greedy longings of the mind) and the pride of life (assurance in one's own resources or in the stability of earthly things) — these do not come from the Father but are from the world (itself)" (1 Jn 2:16). These three wounds destroy the original harmony we once shared with God and His creation in the garden. The greater one's attachment is to these worldly desires, the more detached one becomes to God's will and God's Divine Life.

This triple slavery, which replaces the original harmony, is order overthrown. Christ came to restore the order that had been destroyed; with this end in view, He gave us the three *evangelical counsels* (or counsels of perfection). The Catechism of the Catholic Church teaches that these virtues have a clear application to everyone who aspires to a life of discipleship.

Poverty (counters lust of the eyes): In the face of a materialistic, consumer culture where one's value is often determined by earning power or the acquisition of wealth, a spirit of poverty testifies to our dependence upon God as the source of all gifts and our solidarity with one another, especially the poor. What does it mean to be "poor in spirit"? In Matthew 13:44 Jesus tells this parable: "The kingdom of heaven is like a treasure buried in a field, which a person finds and hides again, and out of joy goes and sells all that he has and buys that field." To be poor in spirit is to realize that nothing we have is worth more than the kingdom of God. Knowing this, we become willing to part with anything we have if it hinders us from receiving the kingdom. This is why Jesus said, "No one of you can be My disciple who does not give up all his own possessions" (Lk 14:33). Being poor in spirit does not always mean taking vows of poverty or despising the blessings God has given us. Instead, it is a condition of the heart. The main point is always "detachment." It's not whether you have it or not, it's how you have it.

Chastity (counters lust of the flesh): Chastity is a commitment to purity and fidelity no matter what your state in life, whether married, single, or consecrated. Sex is used in our society for so many purposes, including the selling of products and recreation, and the prevailing message is that one must be sexually active to be fully human — even if that means promiscuity. Chastity reminds us of the deeper meaning of sexuality. Those who are reverent and respectful toward their bodies and those of others, with God's grace, will maintain their purity. Many in society treat people like animals and detach the "marital act" from the reverence it deserves. They accept it and promote it in the wrong context and thus betray its sacredness.

Obedience (counters pride of life): Obedience actually means the practice of listening. It is a commitment to listen to God through the mediation of Sacred Scripture and through the teaching of Christ's Bride, the Church. We choose obedience to indicate a preference for the common good over personal desire. The modern-day definition of freedom is to be able to do whatever one wants to do as long as it does not interfere with the rights of others — freedom from responsibility. Obedience demonstrates that the most perfect form of freedom is that which makes a commitment to another person (divine or human) or a cause.

Impressive warrior saints like St. Francis of Assisi taught these counsels of perfection by wearing a rope around their waist with three knots in it; each knot would denote poverty, chastity, and obedience. Today, some have followed their lead by wearing a small rope around their wrists with these three knots, reminding them how to be free, no longer tied to the world but to God. Are you *free to enlist* in Christ's elite fighting force and be the warrior saint He is calling you to be?

PART TWO:
BASIC TRAINING

PART TWO: BASIC TRAINING

2-1. Warrior Ethos

The Soldier's Creed of the United States Army states: "I am disciplined, physically and mentally tough, trained and proficient in my warrior tasks and drills."[39] Former Navy SEAL Eric Greitens said: "One of the things that makes a warrior into a warrior is that they are dedicated to developing their strength in service to others."[40]

Whether it's a Navy SEAL or a Saint, we admire those who put it all on the line — go "all in!" — those who are totally dedicated to the mission. In the military, this dedication is revealed in the Warrior Ethos, four simple lines embedded in the Soldier's Creed:

✠ I will always place the mission first.

✠ I will never accept defeat.

✠ I will never quit.

✠ I will never leave a fallen comrade.

Sustained and developed through discipline, commitment, and pride, these four lines motivate every soldier to persevere and, ultimately, to refuse defeat. What would happen if we dedicated ourselves to the training and mission of Jesus Christ with the same intensity Eric Greitens and his comrades dedicated themselves to the "Warrior Ethos" and to their training to become Navy SEALs? What is keeping us from becoming, in essence, SEALS for Christ?

This section of your Field Manual will test you in your resolve to become strong in the Lord and His mighty power. You will also learn the special operations (special ops) techniques and procedures for search and rescue missions of fallen comrades (those who have become weak in their faith). Although rarely wielded by Catholics today, this supernatural strength and these techniques are truly authentic gifts of the Church that are field-tested and battle-hardened. We must commit ourselves to their restoration if we ever hope to stem the tide of evil and rescue our lost loved ones who may be destined for eternal damnation.

2-2. You are a Commissioned Officer

Admission into Christ's elite fighting force begins by knowing that by your Baptism you have been "commissioned by the Lord Jesus Christ to fulfill a most dramatic mission; it is the mission of saving souls. This mission cannot be accomplished without entering into conflict with 'the world, the flesh, and the devil.' It is not a mission for the fainthearted or for those who wish to take the wide road to heaven. It is the path of warfare, of spiritual battle."[41]

"Holiness," writes Pope Benedict XVI, "has its deepest root in the grace of Baptism, in being grafted on to the Paschal Mystery of Christ, by which His Spirit is communicated to us, His very life as the Risen One."[42] Jesus Christ is the one Whom the Father anointed with the Holy Spirit and established as priest, prophet, and king. The whole People of God participates in these *three offices of Christ* and bears the responsibilities for mission and service that flow from them (CCC 783).

In St. Faustina's Diary (742), our Lord put it this way:

> "I am giving you three ways of exercising mercy toward your neighbor: the first — by deed, the second — by word, the third — by prayer. In these three degrees is contained the fullness of mercy, and it is an unquestionable proof of love of me."[43]

Notice how these three degrees of mercy — prayer, word, and deed — are present in the corresponding offices of priest, prophet, and king. From the very first days of our membership in the Mystical Body of Christ, we are, in essence, *commissioned officers in the Church Militant.* In other words, the power of the Holy Spirit to combat evil and rescue souls proceeds precisely through the three offices of Christ: Priest, Prophet, and King.

Priest: Fr. Robert Barron says "A priest prays for others, intercedes, and performs sacrifices. ... Priests are border walkers. They walk the border between heaven and earth. They are mediators. They're friends of God and friends of the human race. They bring divinity and humanity together. ... It means you must be a person of prayer — intercessory prayer — prayer on behalf of the people of God. It pleases God to channel His providential care precisely through us and through the instrumentality of our prayer."[44]

Recall the last line of the Warrior Ethos: "I will never leave a fallen comrade." When I read this, I think of recent Medal of Honor recipients who reportedly ran through a hail of bullets to rescue their comrades from the clutches of the enemy. It is very similar in the spiritual realm. When our loved ones are "dead in sin," they are not only separated from God, but they lose their desire to seek God. Some become so far removed from God that they find repulsive all things spiritual. So, prayer, Holy Mass, spiritual reading, etc. all become boring and, to some, even detestable when they are dead inside: no Divine Life. They are, quite literally, caught behind enemy lines (imprisoned in their worldliness) with no way out unless some campaign of search and rescue is launched. Does our love, care, and concern for them extend to their eternal salvation? Remember the Warrior Ethos: "I will never leave a fallen comrade!"

St. John Vianney understood this critical need to call out to God in prayer on behalf of those caught in the clutches of the enemy and unable to save themselves:

> "I can't stop praying for poor sinners who are on the road to hell. If they come to die in that state, they will be lost for all eternity. What a pity! We have to pray for sinners! Praying for sinners is the most beautiful and useful of prayers because the just are on the way to heaven, the souls of purgatory are sure to enter there, but the poor sinners will be lost forever. *All devotions are good but there is no better one than such prayer for sinners.* What souls we can convert by our prayers ... Not only would one contribute to God's glory by this holy practice of praying for sinners, but one would obtain an abundance of grace. I am only content when I'm praying for sinners. The good God has made me see how much He loves that I pray for poor sinners. I don't know if it were really a voice I heard or a dream, but, whatever it was, it woke me up and told me that to save a soul in the state of sin is more pleasing to God than all sacrifices. For that reason, I do all my resolutions for penance" (emphasis added).

The only approved apparition of the Blessed Mother in the United States occurred right near Coach Vince Lombardi's Green Bay, Wisconsin, in the town of Champion, and is known as Our Lady of Good Help. The message given by our Lady on October 9, 1859, was: "I am the Queen of Heaven, who prays for the conversion of sinners, and I wish you to do the same." How much clearer could it be that *praying* for poor sinners (loved ones who have lost the gift of faith) must rank among the highest things in our devotional life?

Prophet: Fr. Robert Barron says, "A prophet is someone who speaks for God. ... Their task was to speak God's word, in season and out. When that word was popular; when it was not. ... (It means you should be a reader) of theology and spirituality ... that you might, as St. Peter put it, be able to 'give a reason for the hope that is in you.' ... We're living in a time when religion is under attack. ... If someone challenged you, could you give a reason for the hope that is in you?"[45]

For Pope Leo XIII, to be a prophet means we are *"born for combat"*: "'To recoil before an enemy, or to keep silence when from all sides such clamors are raised against truth,' he warns, 'is the part of a man either devoid of character or who entertains doubt as to the truth of what he professes to believe.' The only ones who win when Christians stay quiet, he says, are the enemies of truth. The silence of Catholics is particularly disturbing because frequently a few bold words would have vanquished the false ideas. 'Christians are,' Leo continues, 'born for combat.' It is part of their nature to follow Christ by espousing unpopular ideas and by defending the truth at great cost to themselves."[46]

The element of surprise often catches us off-guard when faced with an opportunity to defend the faith from attacks or share why our faith is so important to us. Those moments often come and go rather quickly. These can be seen as "teaching moments" as they teach us to be better prepared the next time it happens. This is why it is essential for us to make the necessary preparations by developing short but impactful statements or quotes that really leave, in a brief moment, a spiritual mark on the recipients. In the public relations world, these are called

talking points or, as Pope Leo XIII called them, "a few bold
words." A talking point in debate or discourse is a
succinct statement designed to persuasively support one
side taken on an issue. Such statements can either be free
standing or created as retorts to the opposition's talking
points. Yes, you should study theology and spirituality,
but like arrows in your quiver, you must have these
talking points prepared and memorized, ready to fire.
More than anything else, before ever opening your
mouth, take a deep breath and ask the Holy Spirit to
speak through you in love.

King: A king is someone who *leads* others to God. A
good king is someone who leads by example. A good king
is someone who puts those in his charge ahead of himself.
Christ the King said, "I have not come to be served, but to
serve." And then He got down on His hands and knees and
washed the dirty feet of His disciples. He told them, "You
want to be great? Then be the slave of the rest" (Mt
20:27-28, Jn 13:4-5).

As Jean-Baptiste Chautard recounts in his book *The Soul
of the Apostolate,* Pope St. Pius X was conversing with a
group of his cardinals one day. The pope asked them:

"What is the thing we most need, today, to save
society?"
"Build Catholic schools," said one.
"No."
"More churches," said another.
"Still no."
"Speed up the recruiting of priests," said a third.
"No, no," said the pope, "the *most* necessary thing of all,
at this time, is for every parish to possess a group of
laymen who will be at the same time virtuous,
enlightened, resolute, and truly apostolic."

Chautard continues, "Further details enable us to assert
that this holy pope at the end of his life saw no hope for

the salvation of the world unless the clergy could use their zeal to form faithful Christians full of apostolic ardor, preaching by word and example, but especially by example. In the diocese where he served before being elevated to the papacy, he attached less importance to the (count) of parishioners than to the list of Christians capable of radiating an apostolate. It was his opinion that *shock troops could be formed in any environment*" (emphasis added).[47]

"Shock troops" (or assault troops) is actually a military term that refers to infantry formations, along with supporting units, created to lead an attack. Consider the Allied Forces of World War II moving toward the beaches of Normandy on D-Day, June 6, 1944. That first wave of men knew full well that their chances were extremely poor of ever leaving that beach alive, but they knew somebody needed to go first. It is no less than profound that the holy Pope St. Pius X would use a military term, *shock troops,* to describe the most necessary need of our times. The pope is resolute in acknowledging we are in spiritual warfare as he calls for an uncommon valor willing to be the tip of the spear, *the vanguard,* warrior saints unafraid "to lead."

2-3. Go Weapons Hot

"Go Weapons Hot" is a military command that means to make whatever preparations are necessary so that when you pull the trigger, something happens. In spiritual terms, are we using live ammunition or are we firing blanks? In other words, are we making the preparations necessary to ensure that our efforts to combat evil and rescue souls are ignited by the fire of the Holy Spirit? As a Commissioned Officer in the Church Militant, am I imploring God to *supernaturally weaponize* my prayers (priest), words (prophet), and deeds (king) so that "I can do all things through Christ Who gives me strength" (Phil 4:13)? Or am I ignoring His supernatural strength and power and, therefore, firing blanks — "We've been hard at it all night and have caught nothing" (Lk 5:5)?

What are the preparations necessary so that "something (effective) happens" as we exercise the three offices of Christ in the war "against the principalities and powers, the rulers of this world of darkness, the evil spirits in regions above" (Eph 6:10-12)? The word "hot" ("Go Weapons Hot") gives us an excellent acronym for understanding how we are best positioned to receive the free offer of God's supernatural grace: H.O.T. = **H**umility, **O**bedience, **T**rust.

Humility: St. Ignatius of Loyola said, "There is no doubt that God will never be wanting to us, provided that He finds in us that humility which makes us worthy of His gifts, the desire of possessing them, and the promptitude to co-operate industriously with the graces He gives us."

Obedience: St. Josemaria Escriva wrote, "The power of obedience! The lake of Genesareth had denied its fishes to Peter's nets. A whole night in vain. Then, obedient, he lowered his net again to the water and they caught 'a huge number of fish.' Believe me: the miracle is repeated each day."[48]

Trust: St. Alphonsus Liguori taught, "He who trusts himself is lost. He who trusts in God can do all things." The most important aspect of the devotion of Divine Mercy is the need to trust in God's goodness. Jesus revealed to St. Faustina that *"the vessel with which souls receive abundant graces, and special favors, is confidence!"* The confident, trusting soul is like a lightning rod for God's mercy and grace.

2-4. Confession: God's Confidence Course

In the Marine Corps Basic Training, recruits must execute a motivational exercise called the "Confidence Course." "It's really a confidence booster," said Staff Sgt. Roger Taylor, close combat instructor, Instructional Training Company. "Confidence Course II is where the recruits tackle all the high obstacles ... Some recruits are terrified of heights, and sometimes, recruits don't know they are scared of heights until they get up. But we encourage and motivate them to complete the obstacles, and once they do, it's a great sense of accomplishment, and they leave ... ready to take on any challenge."[49]

In the spiritual life, the challenge to climb new heights is always before us. Our willingness to ascend to meet God builds the confidence we need to take on the challenges He will set before those who trust Him. "Therefore, let us go forth with confidence toward the throne of grace, so that we may obtain mercy, and find grace, in a helpful time" (Heb 4:16).

Pope Benedict XVI reminds us of the conditions for this ascent: "Inquiring after God, seeking His face — that is the first and fundamental condition for ascent that leads to the encounter with God."[50] He goes on to point out that even before that, however, Psalm 24 specifies clean hands and a pure heart: "Who shall ascend the hill of the Lord? And who shall stand in His holy place? He who has clean hands and a pure heart, who does not lift his soul to what is false, and does not swear deceitfully" (Ps 24:3-4).

Approaching the throne of God is an amazing thing, but make no mistake about it, it is also a challenging thing. God is light and truth. Drawing nearer to God's light shines more light on ourselves and all of those blotches and blemishes (disobedience and sin) we thought we could conceal:

"For the Word of God is living and effective: more piercing than any two-edged sword, reaching to the division even between the soul and the spirit, even between the joints and the marrow, and so it discerns the thoughts and intentions of the heart. And there is no created thing that is invisible to His sight. For all things are naked and open to the eyes of Him, about Whom we are speaking" (Heb 4:12-13).

Throughout the Bible we see those who, once they realize they are in the presence of the Divine, become troubled and some recoil with words such as, "Leave me Lord, for I am a sinful man" (Lk 5:8). They know that Divinity can see what can remain concealed to humanity. At once, they require reassurance: "Do not be afraid" (Lk 5:9-10).

As difficult as it may seem to expose our blotches to God, we know that we have a sympathetic High Priest Who wants nothing more for us than to gain us access to the throne of grace:

"Therefore, since we have a great High Priest, Who has pierced the heavens, Jesus the Son of God, we should hold to our confession. For we do not have a high priest who is unable to have compassion on our infirmities, but rather one who was tempted in all things, just as we are, yet without sin" (Heb 4:14-15).

St. Josemaria Escriva wrote: "What security should be ours in considering the mercy of the Lord! 'He has but to cry for redress, and I, the ever merciful, will listen to him' (Ex 22:27). It is an invitation, a promise that He will not fail to fulfill. 'Let us then with confidence draw near to the throne of grace, and we may receive mercy and find grace to help in time of need' (Heb 4:16). The enemies of our sanctification will be rendered powerless if the mercy of God goes before us. And if through our own fault and human weakness we should fall, the Lord comes to our aid and raises us up."[51]

We have a Divine Physician Who desires to remove all of the spiritual blocks of sin and disobedience that inhibit the free flow of Divine Life into us. These blocks are like the plaque that can build up in arteries, restricting blood flow to the heart. St. Thomas Aquinas said: "In the life of the body a man is sometimes sick, and unless he takes medicine, he will die. Even so in the spiritual life a man is sick on account of sin. For that reason he needs medicine so that he may be restored to health; and this grace is bestowed in the Sacrament of Penance."

"The whole power of the Sacrament of Penance consists in restoring us to God's grace and joining us with Him in an intimate friendship."[52] St. Augustine tells us: "This very moment I may, if I desire, become the friend of God." Indeed the Sacrament of Reconciliation with God brings about a true "spiritual resurrection," restoration of the dignity and blessings of the life of the children of God, of which the most precious is friendship with God (Lk 15:32).

For those who partake in frequent Confession — at least once a month — they have come to understand the restorative and refreshing value of this practice. Pope John Paul II (who went to Confession weekly) taught: "It would be an illusion to want to strive for holiness in accordance with the vocation that God has given to each one of us without frequently and fervently receiving this sacrament of conversion and sanctification."[53] Those who go to Confession frequently, and do so with the desire to make progress, will notice the strides that they make in their spiritual lives.

The procedure for making a good Confession is found on page 152. Also, questions for an examination of conscience are found on page 153.

2-5. Top Secret to Happiness

Surveys by Gallup, the National Opinion Research Center, and the Pew Organization conclude that spiritually committed people are twice as likely to report being "very happy" than the least religiously committed people. Secular analysts seem to be doing back flips trying to explain away the simple reality that there is no other authentic and fulfilling way to live other than a supernatural life.

St. Paul writes, "The unspiritual man does not receive the gifts of the Spirit of God, for they are foolishness to him, and he is not able to understand them because they are spiritually discerned" (1 Cor 2:14). This is the person who acts only by using his or her human faculties (intelligence and will) and who therefore can be wise only in the things of the world. He remains superficial and worldly. This is a heart that has hardened to the presence of God. The prophet Jeremiah writes "Cursed is the man who trusts in human beings, who seeks his strength in flesh, whose heart turns away from the Lord. He is like a barren bush in the desert that enjoys no change of season, but stands in a lava waste, a salt land and empty earth" (Jer 17:5-6).

However, throughout the Bible (e.g., Ps 1, Jer 17, Rev 22) we are told that the blessed ones are those who trust God and His ordinances; they are like trees planted beside streams of water. These trees are full of life (their leaves stay green) and they fulfill their purpose (produce fruit) even in the face of life's challenges. The Navarre Bible comments, "The spiritual man is the Christian reborn by the grace of God; grace elevates his faculties to enable him to perform actions which have a supernatural value — acts of faith, hope, and charity. A person who is in the state of grace is able to perceive the things of God, because he carries with him the Spirit in his soul in grace, and he has Christ's mind, Christ's attitude. 'We have no alternative,' St. Josemaria Escriva teaches, 'there are only two possible ways of living on this earth: either we live a supernatural life, or we live an animal life. And you and I can only live the life of God, a supernatural life' (*Friends of God*)."54

If you sincerely want this power, energy, life, and strength, you have to stand near Him. You have to be around what He breathes forth: The Holy Spirit. So, if you want the power of the Holy Spirit, you have to declare the Lordship of Jesus Christ and you need to be near Him as He breathes out this power, which is Divine Love. You must abide in Him. Like Mary, you must look Him in the eye — Face to Face — and love Him. You must give Him the very same precious gift you give anyone you truly love: *Time*. The secret to holiness and friendship with God is constant prayer: "Pray always and do not lose heart" (Lk 18:1).

2-6. Store up Spiritual Energy

The heroes of our faith are the warrior saints who have gone before us. God worked mightily and miraculously through them. Therefore, we must study their ways. In humility, obedience, and trust (H.O.T.), we ask: How did they remain so well connected, in such strong friendship with God, so that His river of supernatural grace could flow so freely through them? What do these "SEALS for Christ" teach us about the ideal spiritual disciplines, the ultimate daily regimen of prayer?

"Pray with great confidence," St. Louis de Montfort says, "with confidence based upon the goodness and infinite generosity of God and upon the promises of Jesus Christ. God is a spring of living water that flows unceasingly into the hearts of those who pray."

Prayer is our outstanding supernatural resource for fighting the wiles of the enemy. St. Alphonsus said, "Prayer is, beyond doubt, the most powerful weapon the Lord gives us to conquer evil ... but we must really put ourselves into the prayer, it is not enough just to say the words, it must come from the heart. And also prayer needs to be continuous, we must pray no matter what kind of situation we find ourselves in: the warfare we are engaged in is ongoing, so our prayer must be on-going also."

The following are largely based on Fr. John McCloskey's *Seven Daily Habits of Holy Apostolic People* and include:

1. The Morning Offering
2. Mental Prayer (at least 15 minutes)
3. Spiritual Reading (at least 15 minutes)
4. Holy Mass and Communion
5. The Angelus (at noon)
6. The Holy Rosary
7. Brief Examination of Conscience (at night)

Father McCloskey writes: "These are the principal means to achieve holiness. If you are a person who wants to bring Christ to others through your friendship, these are the instruments by which you store up the spiritual energy that will enable you to do so. Apostolic action without the sacraments and a deep solid interior life will in the long run be ineffective. You can be sure that all the saints incorporated in one way or another all of these habits into their daily routine. Your goal is to be like them, contemplatives in the middle of the world."[55]

We are being asked to allow God's grace to surge through us to a waiting world, but *nemo dat quod non habet* (no one gives what he does not have). Father McCloskey correctly points out that these exceptional habits of prayer are the way of *storing up spiritual energy* to be used to bring Christ to others. St. Bernadette said: "Do not just be a channel for grace, but a reservoir, an overflowing reservoir. No sooner has a channel received grace than it pours it out. A reservoir waits to be filled up and then offers grace to those who come to draw from its superabundance."

Let's consider some key points before we look more closely at each of these seven daily habits:

First, just like someone who is starting a daily exercise program, you don't go out and run several miles on the first day. That would invite failure, and God wants to see you succeed. Take it easy on yourself as you incorporate these habits in your daily routine over time. Consider using the 12-Week Church Militant Boot Camp starting on page 123 as a very effective way to get your robust interior life up and running.

Second, while gradually implementing these habits, you still want to make a firm commitment, with the help of the Holy Spirit, to make them *the* priority in your life — more important than meals, sleep, work, and recreation.

Third, St. Basil writes, "The reason why sometimes you have asked and not received is because you have asked amiss, either inconsistently, or lightly, or because you have asked for what was not good for you, or because you have ceased asking." It is time to set aside the undisciplined, "free-styling" way in which most of us have practiced our daily prayer life throughout our lives. The *cult of the casual* has become so pervasive in the world that it has seeped into our faith lives. This lack of discipline has spelled disaster for those who have ever attempted to maintain regular habits of prayer. These habits must be done when we are most alert, during the day, in a place that is silent and without distractions, where it is easy to put ourselves in God's presence and address Him. Schedule your prayer or it will never happen.

Fourth, Father McCloskey points out that "living the seven daily habits is not a zero sum game. You are not losing time but rather, in reality, gaining it. I have never met a person who lived them on a daily basis who became a less productive worker as a result, or a worse spouse, or who had less time for his friends, or could no longer grow in his cultural life. Quite the contrary, God always rewards those who put Him first. Our Lord will multiply our time amazingly as He did with those few loaves and fishes that fed the multitude with plenty left over."[56]

1. Morning Offering: This is a prayer that lets you begin by offering up your entire day for the glory of God. While there are many formulas for this short prayer, I recommend the one on page 147, as this vintage version includes a plea to seek the indulgences offered that day. St. Josemaria Escriva also encourages us to get up on the dot: "Conquer yourself each day from the very first moment, getting up on the dot, at a set time, without granting a single minute to laziness. If with the help of God, you conquer yourself in the moment, you have accomplished a great deal for the rest of the day. It's so discouraging to find yourself beaten in the first skirmish."[57] This is called the "heroic moment" and gives us the physical and spiritual energy throughout the day to stop what we are doing in order to live the other habits. Once your feet hit the ground, speak the words "I will serve!" (or *Serviam*, in Latin).

2. Mental Prayer (15 minutes): This is "face time," the "one thing necessary" *(unum necessarium)* that constitutes the essential foundation for the interior life. This prayer is simply one-on-one direct conversation with Jesus Christ, preferably before the Blessed Sacrament in the tabernacle. A brief description is found on page 149.

3. Spiritual Reading (15 minutes): This refers to the systematic reading of Sacred Scripture known as Lectio Divina (see page 150) as well as the classic understanding of spiritual reading that is devoted to the reading of lives of saints, writings of Doctors and the Fathers of the Church, and other works written by holy people. As St. Josemaria Escriva puts it, "Don't neglect your spiritual reading. Reading has made many saints."[58]

4. Hear Daily Holy Mass and Receive Holy Communion: This is the most important habit of all the seven. As such, it has to be at the very center of our interior life and consequently our day. St. Peter Julian Eymard tells us to "hear Mass daily; it will prosper the whole day. All your duties will be performed the better for it, and your soul will be stronger to bear its daily cross. The Mass is the most holy act of religion; you can do nothing that can give greater glory to God or be more profitable for your soul than to hear Mass both frequently and devoutly. It is the favorite devotion of the saints."

5. Angelus (or Regina Coeli): This is the very ancient Catholic custom that has us stop what we are doing to greet our Blessed Mother for a moment (at 6:00 a.m., 12:00 noon, and 6:00 p.m. daily), as any good child remembers his mother during the day, and to meditate on the Incarnation and Resurrection of our Lord, which give such meaning to our entire existence. The Regina Coeli is said during the Easter season. The Angelus is said during the rest of the year. See page 148 for these prayers.

6. Holy Rosary: As St. Josemaria Escriva puts it, "For those who use their intelligence and their study as a weapon, the Rosary is most effective, because this apparently monotonous way of beseeching Our Lady, as children do their mother, can destroy every seed of vainglory and pride."[59] Father McCloskey reminds us that "by repeating words of love to Mary and offering up each decade for our intentions, we take the shortcut to Jesus, which is to pass through the heart of Mary. He cannot refuse her anything!"[60] Pope Pius IX once said, "Give me an army saying the Rosary and I will conquer the world." See page 201 for step-by-step instructions for praying the Rosary.

7. Nightly Examination of Conscience: Take a few minutes just before bed to review your day asking, "How have I behaved as a child of God?" It's also a great time to look at that "dominant fault" you need to improve upon in order to become a saint. Conclude these few minutes of reflection by praying three Hail Marys for purity and then pray the "Act of Contrition" (page 151).

PART THREE:
SEARCH AND RESCUE

PART THREE:
SEARCH AND RESCUE

3-1. "I've Got Your Six!"

"The fervent petition of a holy man is powerful indeed. My brothers, the case may arise among you of someone straying from the truth and of another bringing him back. Remember this: the person who brings a sinner back from his way will save his soul from death and cancel a multitude of sins" (Jas 5:16b, 19-20).

"I've got your six" is a military phrase that basically means "I've got your back." It comes from the old pilot system in which directions correspond to hours on the clock, where 12 o'clock is forward and 6 o'clock is behind. Thus anyone behind you is "at your six."

Blessed Peter Favre said, "I felt great desires that the saints might pray for us, they who have so much power in their state of glory, and that the souls in purgatory might offer prayers for us amidst those remorseful lamentations of theirs ... these souls can do much for us (more than we can tell)." St. John Vianney said, "Oh! If all of us but knew how great is the power of the good souls in purgatory with the heart of God, and if we knew all the graces we can attain through their intercession, they would not be so much forgotten! We must pray much for them, so that they may pray much for us."

We are not meant to advance unaided. In His great wisdom, God has set up a Holy Alliance that, once united, is designed to defeat any and all forces of darkness in the heavenly realm, rescue souls, and build up the kingdom of God. This alliance is the aforementioned Communion of Saints. It is the exchange of the *Sancta Sanctis*! ("God's holy gifts for God's holy people!") Those on earth (Church Militant) invoke the saints in heaven and pray for the souls in purgatory (we can gain indulgences for them). When called upon, those in heaven pray for the Church Militant and the Church Penitent; they obtain graces for us on earth and an alleviation of suffering for the poor souls in purgatory. Those in purgatory can, when called upon, invoke the saints on high and pray for us struggling with the world, the flesh, and the evil spirit.

St. Thomas Aquinas wrote: "Charity is incomplete until it includes the dead as well as the living." While we live together on earth as Christians, we are in communion, or unity, with one another. But that communion doesn't end when one of us dies. In the Communion of Saints "a perennial link of charity exists between the faithful who have already reached their heavenly home, those who are expiating their sins in purgatory, and those who are still pilgrims on earth. Between them there is, too, an abundant exchange of all good things."[61] In other words, the bond of love remains, along with the self-emptying nature of that real love. Even separated by death, we continue to care for each other, look out for each other, and build each other up. And so we continue to say to one another, "I've got your six!"

To understand how God's amazing structure for this loving exchange of spiritual goods is built, we must learn what we mean by indulgences. St. Ignatius of Loyola wrote, "Indulgences are of such value that I find myself unable to appreciate them according to their true worth or to speak of them highly enough. Thus I exhort you to hold them in the highest possible esteem."

3-2. Indulgences 101

In the last days of Pope John Paul II's pontificate, he met with some American bishops in May of 2004 and recommended that U.S. Catholics recover "devotions of popular piety" as a means of "personal and communal sanctification."[62] Sadly, many wonderful Catholic devotional treasures had been discarded, by and large, during the rebellious days following the Council of Vatican II. But, by the grace of God, the practice of gaining indulgences for ourselves and the holy souls in purgatory is being restored.

Catholic Answers' *Primer on Indulgences* teaches:

"Those who claim that indulgences are no longer part of Church teaching have the admirable desire to distance themselves from abuses that occurred around the time of the Protestant Reformation. They also want to remove stumbling blocks that prevent non-Catholics from taking a positive view of the Church. As admirable as these motives are, the claim that indulgences are not part of Church teaching today is false. This is proved by the Catechism of the Catholic Church, which states, 'An indulgence is obtained through the Church who, by virtue of the power of binding and loosing granted her by Christ Jesus, intervenes in favor of individual Christians and opens for them the treasury of the merits of Christ and the saints to obtain from the Father of mercies the remission of the temporal punishment due for their sins.' The Church does this not just to aid Christians, 'but also to spur them to works of devotion, penance, and charity' (CCC 1478)."[63]

What is an indulgence? The word comes from the Latin *indulgentia*, which means "to be kind or tender." "To understand what an indulgence is," writes contemporary author Steve Kellmeyer, "we have to know what our sin does to the world and ourselves. When we commit sin, two things happen. First, we kill the life of grace within us. This deserves punishment. Spiritually, a sinner is a dead man, walking. Second, by removing grace from ourselves, we also remove grace from the created universe. Thus, each sin, no matter how venial, attacks both the moral order of the universe and the very material of creation itself."[64]

The following explanation of indulgences comes from Steve Kellmeyer's *Calendar of Indulgences*:

> "**Forgiveness:** When God pours out mercy in the Sacrament of Reconciliation, He does something we have no right to expect — He forgives our sins and restores the life of grace within us, resurrecting us from death. As a result, we must act (penance) to change our life and renew our way of living (amendment of life). However, though we have been resurrected, we still deserve punishment for the attack we made on God's creation. Further, the horrible consequences of our attack, which removed grace from creation, continue to affect the world even if we ourselves have been healed through the sacrament. God expects us to help repair the damage.

> "**Repair Work:** We can do this repair work either here on earth or in purgatory. Since God intended us to live with our bodies united to our souls, it is much easier to do this repair work here. In purgatory, our soul and body are separate. The suffering of purgatory is always much more painful than suffering on earth because it is harder to do the necessary repair work when the body isn't around to help.

"**The Storehouse:** Cardinal John Newman said, 'The smallest venial sin rocks the foundations of the created world.' That is, even our smallest sin can cause devastating consequences in creation; famine, disease, natural disaster. However, through God's grace, the holiness of even the lowliest saint far exceeds the harm even the greatest sinner can do. Further, Christ's work on the cross is infinitely greater in merit than that of the greatest saint in Christendom, the Blessed Virgin Mary. Thus, the graces won by Christ and the saints are an infinite treasure that can be used to heal the wounds of the world. God intends us to use this treasury — indeed; we could not help wipe out the effects of our sin without the divine treasury God established. *An indulgence, then, applies the graces won by Christ and the saints to the world so as to heal the wounds I caused by my sins.*

"A plenary indulgence heals all of the effects of one person's sins. A partial indulgence heals part of the effects. One can win indulgences only for oneself or those in purgatory who have need of assistance because they currently lack bodies. Indulgences cannot be applied towards other living persons. Every living person is supposed to do his own acts of obedience to help heal the worldly effects of his own sinfulness (CCC 1471-1473)."[65]

Requirements for obtaining a plenary indulgence:

✠ Do the work while in a state of grace

✠ Receive sacramental Confession within 20 days of the work (several plenary indulgences may be earned per reception)

✠ Receive Eucharistic communion (one plenary indulgence may be earned per reception of Eucharist)

✠ Pray for the pope's intentions (an Our Father and Hail Mary, or other appropriate prayer, is sufficient)

✠ Have no attachment to sin (even venial) — i.e., the Christian makes an act of the will to love God and despise sin.

Requirements for obtaining a partial indulgence:

✠ Do the work while in a state of grace

✠ Have the general intention of earning an indulgence

3-3. Spiritual Strength Conditioning

While Holy Mother Church unlocks her spiritual treasury she, like any good mother, utilizes these prescribed acts of obedience as an occasion to teach her children ("spurs us to works of devotion, penance, and charity" CCC 1478). In other words, when we look at each of the indulgenced good works and prayers granted to us, as well as the conditions necessary for obtaining them, we see that these acts and conditions are the favored ways in which God desires us to grow in holiness, confront evil, and rescue souls.

Consider the conditions required for obtaining a plenary indulgence. If our state in life allows it, the ideal is to obtain one plenary indulgence every day (Mother Church offers one plenary indulgence, and only one, each day). By setting the following conditions, Holy Mother Church is teaching that these conditions reveal what is a rock solid foundation for the interior life:

✠ Sustain and guard your state of grace

✠ Go to Confession frequently (at least once a month)

✠ Hear Daily Mass and receive Communion

✠ Prayer support for our leader (pope)

✠ Free from the slavery of unresolved sin

Like athletes or soldiers dedicated to their training, these "conditions" are our way of maintaining sound spiritual strength conditioning, empowering us to be the qualified contenders God can trust for His missions to battle dark forces and rescue souls. Apart from these basic "conditions," we are weak and vulnerable and God is unlikely to choose us for His missions or bless our endeavors. We are, in essence, sidelined (benched) until we desire to choose His fundamental conditions to get in good spiritual shape.

By elevating certain prayers and good works to the level of gaining an indulgence, Mother Church is identifying which of these she most highly values and, therefore, which ones she urges us to prioritize. This is the best way for us to practice sincere obedience. These indulgenced prayers and good works are all listed in the *Manual of Indulgences* (and easily accessible online). Also, a calendar listing of some plenary indulgences and conditions is available on page 272 of this Field Manual.

3-4. The 'Big Four'

However, we must draw special attention to what I call the "Big Four." Remarkably, Holy Mother Church has elevated only four activities for which a plenary indulgence can be gained on any day (though, as we said, only once a day). Highlighting these four reveals the great esteem in which Mother Church holds them, and, therefore, she urges us to rank these as highest among our daily devotions. The "Big Four" are:

✠ Adoring the Blessed Sacrament for at least 30 minutes

✠ Devoutly reading Sacred Scripture for at least 30 minutes

✠ Devoutly performing the Stations of the Cross

✠ Reciting the Rosary with members of the family, or in a church, oratory, religious community, or pious association

The great significance of the "Big Four" is that Mother Church has provided a way for us to gain that one plenary indulgence every day for ourselves or for a poor soul in purgatory. This then raises the question: Why would we squander this incredibly generous gift? Why wouldn't we accept Mother Church's gracious provision and seek this plenary indulgence every day?

3-5. No Man is an Island

Archbishop Fulton Sheen said, "As we enter heaven we will see them, so many of them coming towards us and thanking us. We will ask who they are, and they will say a poor soul you prayed for in purgatory."

"God has given us the power and privilege," writes best-selling author Susan Tassone, "to relieve and assist the holy souls and hasten their uniting with Him. He places in our hands the means necessary to help them reach heaven. Unless these holy ones are released by the good works of the faithful, God in His ineffable justice is resolved to purify them in purgatory. It is also a duty of personal interest since one day we may expect others to help us in the same way. Souls must undergo purification necessary for heaven, and they beg for our prayers, suffrages, and good works. Their time of personal merit is up. They can do nothing — nothing — for their deliverance. These suffering friends of God cannot do penance. They cannot gain indulgences. They cannot receive the sacraments. They cannot perform new meritorious acts. They depend entirely on our charity. Are we listening?"[66]

Pope Benedict XVI wrote:

"We should recall that no man is an island, entire of itself. Our lives are involved with one another, through innumerable interactions they are linked together. No one lives alone. No one sins alone. No one is saved alone. The lives of others continually spill over into mine: in what I think, say, do, and achieve. And conversely, my life spills over into that of others: for better and for worse. So my prayer for another is not something extraneous to that person, something external, not even after death. In the interconnectedness of Being, my gratitude to the other — my prayer for him — can play a small part in his purification. ... As Christians we should never limit ourselves to asking: How can I save myself? We should also ask: What can I do in order that others may be saved and that for them too the star of hope may rise? Then I will have done my utmost for my own personal salvation as well."[67]

3-6. Building Your Holy Alliance

How many of us had grandparents who had their stack of holy cards in their prayer book? These favorite saints were their friends, their prayer warriors! How many of our ancestors knew to pray for the holy souls in purgatory, especially the souls of family and friends? The holy souls would then, in deep gratitude, return many prayers for those who cared to pray for them. This is why our ancestors never faced evil alone or prayed for anything or anybody alone — they had their comrades in the heavenly realm, their Holy Alliance of saints and holy souls, with them at all times. The devil never stood a chance against this united force!

What's stopping us from building upon the great example of our ancestors who called upon the saints to pray with them for the poor souls in purgatory? If they invoked (recruited) their handful of favorite saints, what's stopping us from building an enormous personal Holy Alliance of saints (as we learn about each one) by recruiting a new saint each day to pray with us? And, while our ancestors had a handful of deceased family and friends for whom they prayed, what's stopping us from going deeper in our family tree (as we learn about each one) by helping more and more generations of our family to reach heaven? These deceased relatives and friends (holy souls) would also be considered recruits in our Holy Alliance as they become "very grateful" holy souls who now pray for us because we prayed for them.

There is something special about invoking (recruiting) each of these saints and holy souls *mano-a-mano* (hand to hand — to give it in person) as opposed to a general calling out for "all the saints" or "all the holy souls." The former is a more loving and personal act of reaching out to each saint and holy soul as we get to know him or her. The latter tends toward more of an impersonal, face-in-the-crowd relationship.

This means that on day one that you begin this practice of praying with a saint for a holy soul in purgatory, you grow from a force of one (just you) to a force of three (the saint you chose, the holy soul you prayed for, and you). On day two, you will add another saint and holy soul to your personal Holy Alliance, and grow to a force of five. And so on.

Different units and formations organize the military. It's interesting to think that, as our Holy Alliance grows, it will be akin to these units:

Your Holy Alliance:

Fire team:	2-4
Squad:	8-13
Platoon:	26-55
Company:	80-225
Battalion:	300-1,300
Regiment:	3,000-5,000
Division:	10,000-15,000

Think about it — inside of six months, you can grow your Holy Alliance to the size of a battalion. Imagine standing before the throne of God, calling out to Him on behalf of a loved one who has lost the precious gift of faith. But now, you do not stand alone — you are standing there with your personal battalion "at your six." Amazing!

3-7. Let's Roll

This is a clarion call to raise an army willing to *"fight for the souls"* of our loved ones. All around us we see one soul after another losing their precious gift of faith. Most of us feel helpless to do anything about it. Our ancestors knew exactly what to do, but the modern Christian has lost the ancient art of "fighting for souls."

In the pages ahead, you will find a Special Ops Search and Rescue Journal that will help you apply all of the principals you have learned in this field manual, such as how to build your own personal army of intercessors by praying for the holy souls and invoking the saints. This personal Holy Alliance will then assist you in rescuing the souls of your living loved ones who are captivated by the world and have lost the gift of faith.

Also, you will find a special 12-Week Church Militant Boot Camp Journal. A boot camp trains soldiers for combat by instilling discipline and an unbreakable bond. When training is complete, soldiers act more as a sacrificing, corporate body and less as self-concerned individuals. You will learn what it means to be God Strong, under His power of grace, and how absolutely essential it is to move in concert, in alliance with the Communion of Saints.

During this Church Militant Boot Camp you will learn the following:

✠ The fundamentals of a quality interior life.

✠ What it means to be commissioned as an officer in the Church Militant.

✠ How to become not just Army Strong but God Strong in the power of His grace.

✠ How to build your own personal army of intercessors by praying for the holy souls and invoking the saints.

✠ The value of the Warrior Ethos: "I will never leave a fallen comrade." Many of our living loved ones are captivated by the world and have lost the gift of faith, and our deceased loved ones wait with longing for our prayers to help them reach heaven.

This is no ordinary army, and therefore, this will be no ordinary training. What is more, we must bear in mind that this is no ordinary adversary we face. Let's once again recall St. Paul's exhortation, "Be strong in the Lord and in His mighty power. Put on the full armor of God, so that you can take your stand against the devil's schemes. For our struggle is not against flesh and blood but against the rulers, against the authorities, against the powers of this dark world, and against the spiritual forces of evil in the heavenly realms" (Eph 6:10-12). LET'S ROLL!

JOURNAL ONE:
SPECIAL OPS
SEARCH & RESCUE

JOURNAL ONE: SPECIAL OPS SEARCH AND RESCUE

This method only orders what we have been practicing together for centuries. It is hoped that this new order offers greater accessibility and spurs more to utilize the *Sancta Sanctis!* ("God's holy gifts for God's holy people!") and pray each other into heaven.

Here is the plan for our daily "special ops mission" of search and rescue:

Step One: Choose a saint and holy soul. First, choose a deceased loved one for whom you wish to pray into heaven. This can be a great nudge to get you to explore your family tree, but you are free to pray for a deceased loved one more than once. Now, choose a saint to pray with you for your deceased loved one. You might choose a saint that was your loved one's favorite saint, or you might pick the patron saint of fishing because your loved one liked to fish, or possibly the saint whose feast it is that day. Look on page 99 of this Field Manual to see a listing of over 400 saints. There is a checkbox alongside each saint's name, which can be a great way for you to keep track of which saints you've recruited into your Holy Alliance. This devotion is a great opportunity to take the time to learn about each saint you are recruiting for your personal Holy Alliance. These days, that's as simple as a quick Internet search to read a paragraph or two about your new recruit.

Step Two: Pray with your saint for your holy soul in purgatory by choosing one of the "Big Four" (Rosary, stations, Scripture, or adoration; see page 271) that allow for a plenary indulgence. Always ask your Guardian Angel to pray with you too. Be sure the conditions are present for receiving a plenary indulgence (again, see page 271). If not, offer a partial indulgence that day for your holy soul in purgatory. (But always try your best to earn that one plenary indulgence offered each day.) Having offered an indulgence for a deceased loved one, that holy soul in purgatory now becomes a "grateful" holy soul who will now offer his/her prayers for you. The St. Gertrude prayer (page 173) is a great way to conclude your prayers.

Step Three: "Never Leave A Fallen Comrade." After completing this indulgenced prayer, ask today's grateful holy soul, today's saint, and all those in your Holy Alliance to join you as you all pray together for a living loved one you believe needs to receive God's grace to grow in faith, hope, and love — who, in some ways, is caught in the clutches of worldliness. Pray the Chaplet of Divine Mercy (see page 250). If the "fallen comrade" (living loved one) is a family member, add the "Prayer for Healing the Family Tree" (see page 181). You are free to pray for a fallen comrade (living loved one) more than once.

This method of search and rescue is what I like to call "Stealth Evangelization" because we, along with our Holy Alliance, are storming the gates of heaven to plead with God to pour out His grace on the fallen comrade (living loved one), and that comrade need not even know what we are up to.

Here is a secret weapon of which many are not aware. Jesus told St. Faustina, "When you say this prayer, with a contrite heart and with faith on behalf of some sinner, I will give him the grace of conversion."[68] This is the prayer:

"O Blood and Water, which gushed forth from the Heart of Jesus as a fount of Mercy for us, I trust in You."

You should pray this prayer at the beginning of your Chaplet of Divine Mercy for your fallen comrade. Also, don't be afraid to pray this "secret weapon prayer" repeatedly, in a stealthy way (inaudibly), for the fallen comrade while you may be seated near him or her. Pray with trust.

The following pages are a convenient journal for you to record your daily "Special Ops" Search and Rescue Mission information.

In the weeks and months ahead, you will be able to look back at this journal and see the names of those who make up your growing Holy Alliance. Then you will certainly know that you are not alone!

How to use the Search and Rescue Journal:

1. Each day choose a deceased loved one (HOLY SOUL) to pray for and a saint (SAINT) to pray with. Write their names in the appropriate columns.

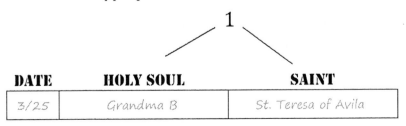

DATE	HOLY SOUL	SAINT
3/25	Grandma B	St. Teresa of Avila

2. Pray and put a check mark in the box next to one of the indulgenced prayers (OFFERING). Determine if the conditions are present for a plenary indulgence. If so, put a check mark next to "Plenary". If not, put a check mark next to "Partial". Refer to page 271 for a quick reference guide for the conditions for plenary indulgences.

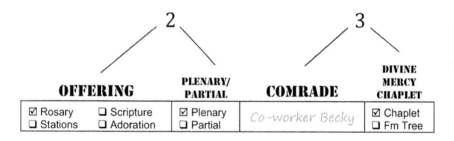

OFFERING		PLENARY/ PARTIAL	COMRADE	DIVINE MERCY CHAPLET
☑ Rosary ☐ Stations	☐ Scripture ☐ Adoration	☑ Plenary ☐ Partial	*Co-worker Becky*	☑ Chaplet ☐ Fm Tree

3. Write the name of a living soul (COMRADE) who is in need of a deepening of their faith, hope, and love. Pray the Divine Mercy Chaplet, and if he or she is a family member, conclude with the Prayer for Healing the Family Tree.

SPECIAL OPS SEARCH AND RESCUE JOURNAL

SEARCH AND RESCUE

DATE	HOLY SOUL	SAINT

SEARCH AND RESCUE

OFFERING		PLENARY/ PARTIAL	COMRADE	DIVINE MERCY CHAPLET
❏ Rosary ❏ Stations	❏ Scripture ❏ Adoration	❏ Plenary ❏ Partial		❏ Chaplet ❏ Fm Tree
❏ Rosary ❏ Stations	❏ Scripture ❏ Adoration	❏ Plenary ❏ Partial		❏ Chaplet ❏ Fm Tree
❏ Rosary ❏ Stations	❏ Scripture ❏ Adoration	❏ Plenary ❏ Partial		❏ Chaplet ❏ Fm Tree
❏ Rosary ❏ Stations	❏ Scripture ❏ Adoration	❏ Plenary ❏ Partial		❏ Chaplet ❏ Fm Tree
❏ Rosary ❏ Stations	❏ Scripture ❏ Adoration	❏ Plenary ❏ Partial		❏ Chaplet ❏ Fm Tree
❏ Rosary ❏ Stations	❏ Scripture ❏ Adoration	❏ Plenary ❏ Partial		❏ Chaplet ❏ Fm Tree
❏ Rosary ❏ Stations	❏ Scripture ❏ Adoration	❏ Plenary ❏ Partial		❏ Chaplet ❏ Fm Tree
❏ Rosary ❏ Stations	❏ Scripture ❏ Adoration	❏ Plenary ❏ Partial		❏ Chaplet ❏ Fm Tree
❏ Rosary ❏ Stations	❏ Scripture ❏ Adoration	❏ Plenary ❏ Partial		❏ Chaplet ❏ Fm Tree
❏ Rosary ❏ Stations	❏ Scripture ❏ Adoration	❏ Plenary ❏ Partial		❏ Chaplet ❏ Fm Tree
❏ Rosary ❏ Stations	❏ Scripture ❏ Adoration	❏ Plenary ❏ Partial		❏ Chaplet ❏ Fm Tree
❏ Rosary ❏ Stations	❏ Scripture ❏ Adoration	❏ Plenary ❏ Partial		❏ Chaplet ❏ Fm Tree
❏ Rosary ❏ Stations	❏ Scripture ❏ Adoration	❏ Plenary ❏ Partial		❏ Chaplet ❏ Fm Tree
❏ Rosary ❏ Stations	❏ Scripture ❏ Adoration	❏ Plenary ❏ Partial		❏ Chaplet ❏ Fm Tree
❏ Rosary ❏ Stations	❏ Scripture ❏ Adoration	❏ Plenary ❏ Partial		❏ Chaplet ❏ Fm Tree
❏ Rosary ❏ Stations	❏ Scripture ❏ Adoration	❏ Plenary ❏ Partial		❏ Chaplet ❏ Fm Tree
❏ Rosary ❏ Stations	❏ Scripture ❏ Adoration	❏ Plenary ❏ Partial		❏ Chaplet ❏ Fm Tree
❏ Rosary ❏ Stations	❏ Scripture ❏ Adoration	❏ Plenary ❏ Partial		❏ Chaplet ❏ Fm Tree
❏ Rosary ❏ Stations	❏ Scripture ❏ Adoration	❏ Plenary ❏ Partial		❏ Chaplet ❏ Fm Tree
❏ Rosary ❏ Stations	❏ Scripture ❏ Adoration	❏ Plenary ❏ Partial		❏ Chaplet ❏ Fm Tree
❏ Rosary ❏ Stations	❏ Scripture ❏ Adoration	❏ Plenary ❏ Partial		❏ Chaplet ❏ Fm Tree

SEARCH AND RESCUE

DATE	HOLY SOUL	SAINT

SEARCH AND RESCUE

OFFERING		PLENARY/ PARTIAL	COMRADE	DIVINE MERCY CHAPLET
❏ Rosary ❏ Stations	❏ Scripture ❏ Adoration	❏ Plenary ❏ Partial		❏ Chaplet ❏ Fm Tree
❏ Rosary ❏ Stations	❏ Scripture ❏ Adoration	❏ Plenary ❏ Partial		❏ Chaplet ❏ Fm Tree
❏ Rosary ❏ Stations	❏ Scripture ❏ Adoration	❏ Plenary ❏ Partial		❏ Chaplet ❏ Fm Tree
❏ Rosary ❏ Stations	❏ Scripture ❏ Adoration	❏ Plenary ❏ Partial		❏ Chaplet ❏ Fm Tree
❏ Rosary ❏ Stations	❏ Scripture ❏ Adoration	❏ Plenary ❏ Partial		❏ Chaplet ❏ Fm Tree
❏ Rosary ❏ Stations	❏ Scripture ❏ Adoration	❏ Plenary ❏ Partial		❏ Chaplet ❏ Fm Tree
❏ Rosary ❏ Stations	❏ Scripture ❏ Adoration	❏ Plenary ❏ Partial		❏ Chaplet ❏ Fm Tree
❏ Rosary ❏ Stations	❏ Scripture ❏ Adoration	❏ Plenary ❏ Partial		❏ Chaplet ❏ Fm Tree
❏ Rosary ❏ Stations	❏ Scripture ❏ Adoration	❏ Plenary ❏ Partial		❏ Chaplet ❏ Fm Tree
❏ Rosary ❏ Stations	❏ Scripture ❏ Adoration	❏ Plenary ❏ Partial		❏ Chaplet ❏ Fm Tree
❏ Rosary ❏ Stations	❏ Scripture ❏ Adoration	❏ Plenary ❏ Partial		❏ Chaplet ❏ Fm Tree
❏ Rosary ❏ Stations	❏ Scripture ❏ Adoration	❏ Plenary ❏ Partial		❏ Chaplet ❏ Fm Tree
❏ Rosary ❏ Stations	❏ Scripture ❏ Adoration	❏ Plenary ❏ Partial		❏ Chaplet ❏ Fm Tree
❏ Rosary ❏ Stations	❏ Scripture ❏ Adoration	❏ Plenary ❏ Partial		❏ Chaplet ❏ Fm Tree
❏ Rosary ❏ Stations	❏ Scripture ❏ Adoration	❏ Plenary ❏ Partial		❏ Chaplet ❏ Fm Tree
❏ Rosary ❏ Stations	❏ Scripture ❏ Adoration	❏ Plenary ❏ Partial		❏ Chaplet ❏ Fm Tree
❏ Rosary ❏ Stations	❏ Scripture ❏ Adoration	❏ Plenary ❏ Partial		❏ Chaplet ❏ Fm Tree
❏ Rosary ❏ Stations	❏ Scripture ❏ Adoration	❏ Plenary ❏ Partial		❏ Chaplet ❏ Fm Tree
❏ Rosary ❏ Stations	❏ Scripture ❏ Adoration	❏ Plenary ❏ Partial		❏ Chaplet ❏ Fm Tree
❏ Rosary ❏ Stations	❏ Scripture ❏ Adoration	❏ Plenary ❏ Partial		❏ Chaplet ❏ Fm Tree
❏ Rosary ❏ Stations	❏ Scripture ❏ Adoration	❏ Plenary ❏ Partial		❏ Chaplet ❏ Fm Tree

SEARCH AND RESCUE

DATE	HOLY SOUL	SAINT

SEARCH AND RESCUE

OFFERING		PLENARY/ PARTIAL	COMRADE	DIVINE MERCY CHAPLET
❑ Rosary ❑ Stations	❑ Scripture ❑ Adoration	❑ Plenary ❑ Partial		❑ Chaplet ❑ Fm Tree
❑ Rosary ❑ Stations	❑ Scripture ❑ Adoration	❑ Plenary ❑ Partial		❑ Chaplet ❑ Fm Tree
❑ Rosary ❑ Stations	❑ Scripture ❑ Adoration	❑ Plenary ❑ Partial		❑ Chaplet ❑ Fm Tree
❑ Rosary ❑ Stations	❑ Scripture ❑ Adoration	❑ Plenary ❑ Partial		❑ Chaplet ❑ Fm Tree
❑ Rosary ❑ Stations	❑ Scripture ❑ Adoration	❑ Plenary ❑ Partial		❑ Chaplet ❑ Fm Tree
❑ Rosary ❑ Stations	❑ Scripture ❑ Adoration	❑ Plenary ❑ Partial		❑ Chaplet ❑ Fm Tree
❑ Rosary ❑ Stations	❑ Scripture ❑ Adoration	❑ Plenary ❑ Partial		❑ Chaplet ❑ Fm Tree
❑ Rosary ❑ Stations	❑ Scripture ❑ Adoration	❑ Plenary ❑ Partial		❑ Chaplet ❑ Fm Tree
❑ Rosary ❑ Stations	❑ Scripture ❑ Adoration	❑ Plenary ❑ Partial		❑ Chaplet ❑ Fm Tree
❑ Rosary ❑ Stations	❑ Scripture ❑ Adoration	❑ Plenary ❑ Partial		❑ Chaplet ❑ Fm Tree
❑ Rosary ❑ Stations	❑ Scripture ❑ Adoration	❑ Plenary ❑ Partial		❑ Chaplet ❑ Fm Tree
❑ Rosary ❑ Stations	❑ Scripture ❑ Adoration	❑ Plenary ❑ Partial		❑ Chaplet ❑ Fm Tree
❑ Rosary ❑ Stations	❑ Scripture ❑ Adoration	❑ Plenary ❑ Partial		❑ Chaplet ❑ Fm Tree
❑ Rosary ❑ Stations	❑ Scripture ❑ Adoration	❑ Plenary ❑ Partial		❑ Chaplet ❑ Fm Tree
❑ Rosary ❑ Stations	❑ Scripture ❑ Adoration	❑ Plenary ❑ Partial		❑ Chaplet ❑ Fm Tree
❑ Rosary ❑ Stations	❑ Scripture ❑ Adoration	❑ Plenary ❑ Partial		❑ Chaplet ❑ Fm Tree
❑ Rosary ❑ Stations	❑ Scripture ❑ Adoration	❑ Plenary ❑ Partial		❑ Chaplet ❑ Fm Tree
❑ Rosary ❑ Stations	❑ Scripture ❑ Adoration	❑ Plenary ❑ Partial		❑ Chaplet ❑ Fm Tree
❑ Rosary ❑ Stations	❑ Scripture ❑ Adoration	❑ Plenary ❑ Partial		❑ Chaplet ❑ Fm Tree
❑ Rosary ❑ Stations	❑ Scripture ❑ Adoration	❑ Plenary ❑ Partial		❑ Chaplet ❑ Fm Tree
❑ Rosary ❑ Stations	❑ Scripture ❑ Adoration	❑ Plenary ❑ Partial		❑ Chaplet ❑ Fm Tree

SEARCH AND RESCUE

DATE	HOLY SOUL	SAINT

SEARCH AND RESCUE

OFFERING		PLENARY/ PARTIAL	COMRADE	DIVINE MERCY CHAPLET
❑ Rosary ❑ Stations	❑ Scripture ❑ Adoration	❑ Plenary ❑ Partial		❑ Chaplet ❑ Fm Tree
❑ Rosary ❑ Stations	❑ Scripture ❑ Adoration	❑ Plenary ❑ Partial		❑ Chaplet ❑ Fm Tree
❑ Rosary ❑ Stations	❑ Scripture ❑ Adoration	❑ Plenary ❑ Partial		❑ Chaplet ❑ Fm Tree
❑ Rosary ❑ Stations	❑ Scripture ❑ Adoration	❑ Plenary ❑ Partial		❑ Chaplet ❑ Fm Tree
❑ Rosary ❑ Stations	❑ Scripture ❑ Adoration	❑ Plenary ❑ Partial		❑ Chaplet ❑ Fm Tree
❑ Rosary ❑ Stations	❑ Scripture ❑ Adoration	❑ Plenary ❑ Partial		❑ Chaplet ❑ Fm Tree
❑ Rosary ❑ Stations	❑ Scripture ❑ Adoration	❑ Plenary ❑ Partial		❑ Chaplet ❑ Fm Tree
❑ Rosary ❑ Stations	❑ Scripture ❑ Adoration	❑ Plenary ❑ Partial		❑ Chaplet ❑ Fm Tree
❑ Rosary ❑ Stations	❑ Scripture ❑ Adoration	❑ Plenary ❑ Partial		❑ Chaplet ❑ Fm Tree
❑ Rosary ❑ Stations	❑ Scripture ❑ Adoration	❑ Plenary ❑ Partial		❑ Chaplet ❑ Fm Tree
❑ Rosary ❑ Stations	❑ Scripture ❑ Adoration	❑ Plenary ❑ Partial		❑ Chaplet ❑ Fm Tree
❑ Rosary ❑ Stations	❑ Scripture ❑ Adoration	❑ Plenary ❑ Partial		❑ Chaplet ❑ Fm Tree
❑ Rosary ❑ Stations	❑ Scripture ❑ Adoration	❑ Plenary ❑ Partial		❑ Chaplet ❑ Fm Tree
❑ Rosary ❑ Stations	❑ Scripture ❑ Adoration	❑ Plenary ❑ Partial		❑ Chaplet ❑ Fm Tree
❑ Rosary ❑ Stations	❑ Scripture ❑ Adoration	❑ Plenary ❑ Partial		❑ Chaplet ❑ Fm Tree
❑ Rosary ❑ Stations	❑ Scripture ❑ Adoration	❑ Plenary ❑ Partial		❑ Chaplet ❑ Fm Tree
❑ Rosary ❑ Stations	❑ Scripture ❑ Adoration	❑ Plenary ❑ Partial		❑ Chaplet ❑ Fm Tree
❑ Rosary ❑ Stations	❑ Scripture ❑ Adoration	❑ Plenary ❑ Partial		❑ Chaplet ❑ Fm Tree
❑ Rosary ❑ Stations	❑ Scripture ❑ Adoration	❑ Plenary ❑ Partial		❑ Chaplet ❑ Fm Tree
❑ Rosary ❑ Stations	❑ Scripture ❑ Adoration	❑ Plenary ❑ Partial		❑ Chaplet ❑ Fm Tree
❑ Rosary ❑ Stations	❑ Scripture ❑ Adoration	❑ Plenary ❑ Partial		❑ Chaplet ❑ Fm Tree
❑ Rosary ❑ Stations	❑ Scripture ❑ Adoration	❑ Plenary ❑ Partial		❑ Chaplet ❑ Fm Tree

SAINTS TO INTERCEDE FOR HOLY SOULS AND COMRADES

A-TEAM SAINTS
- ❑ St. Mary
- ❑ St. Joseph
- ❑ St. Anne
- ❑ St. Joachim
- ❑ St. Michael the Archangel
- ❑ St. Raphael the Archangel
- ❑ St. Gabriel the Archangel

APOSTLES
- ❑ St. Andrew
- ❑ St. Bartholomew
- ❑ St. James the Greater
- ❑ St. James the Less
- ❑ St. John the Evangelist
- ❑ St. Jude
- ❑ St. Matthew
- ❑ St. Matthias
- ❑ St. Peter
- ❑ St. Philip
- ❑ St. Simon
- ❑ St. Thomas

FATHERS OF THE CHURCH
- ❑ St. Alexander
- ❑ St. Barnabas
- ❑ St. Clement of Alexandria
- ❑ St. Clement of Rome
- ❑ St. Cyprian
- ❑ St. Dionysius of Rome
- ❑ St. Ephraim the Syrian
- ❑ St. Gregory Nyssa
- ❑ St. Gregory Thaumaturgus
- ❑ St. Hippolytus
- ❑ St. Ignatius of Antioch
- ❑ St. Irenaeus
- ❑ St. John of Damascus
- ❑ St. Justin Martyr
- ❑ St. Methodius
- ❑ St. Pamphilus
- ❑ St. Papias
- ❑ St. Peter of Alexandria
- ❑ St. Polycarp of Smyrna
- ❑ St. Victorinus
- ❑ St. Vincent of Lerins

DOCTORS OF THE CHURCH
- ❑ St. Ambrose
- ❑ St. Jerome
- ❑ St. Augustine of Hippo
- ❑ St. Gregory the Great
- ❑ St. Athanasius
- ❑ St. Basil the Great
- ❑ St. Gregory Nazianzus
- ❑ St. John Crystostom
- ❑ St. Ephraem
- ❑ St. Hilary of Poitiers
- ❑ St. Cyril of Jerusalem
- ❑ St. Cyril of Alexandria
- ❑ St. Leo the Great
- ❑ St. Peter Chrysologus
- ❑ St. Isidore
- ❑ St. Bede, the Venerable
- ❑ St. John Damascene
- ❑ St. Peter Damian
- ❑ St. Anselm
- ❑ St. Bernard of Clairvaux
- ❑ St. Anthony of Padua
- ❑ St. Albert the Great
- ❑ St. Bonaventure
- ❑ St. Thomas Aquinas
- ❑ St. Catherine of Siena
- ❑ St. Teresa of Jesus of Avila
- ❑ St. Peter Canisius
- ❑ St. John of the Cross
- ❑ St. Robert Bellarmine
- ❑ St. Lawrence of Brindisi

- ☐ St. Francis de Sales
- ☐ St. Alphonsus Ligouri
- ☐ St. Therese of Lisieux
- ☐ St. Hildegard of Bingen
- ☐ St. John of Avila

SAINTS REMEMBERED AT MASS

- ☐ St. Adalbert
- ☐ St. Aloysius Gonzaga
- ☐ St. Andrew Dung-Lac
- ☐ St. Ansgar
- ☐ St. Anthony Mary Zaccaria
- ☐ St. Anthony Mary Claret
- ☐ St. Apollinaris
- ☐ St. Augustine of Canterbury
- ☐ St. Augustine Zhao Rong
- ☐ St. Bernardine of Siena
- ☐ St. Boniface
- ☐ St. Cajetan
- ☐ St. Casmir
- ☐ St. Catherine of Alexandria
- ☐ St. Charles Borromeo
- ☐ St. Christoper Magallanes
- ☐ St. Columban
- ☐ St. Damien Joseph de Veuster
- ☐ St. Eusebius of Vercelli
- ☐ St. Frances Xavier Cabrini
- ☐ St. Francis of Paola
- ☐ St. Francis Xavier
- ☐ St. George
- ☐ St. Henry
- ☐ St. Ignatius of Loyola
- ☐ St. Isaac Jogues
- ☐ St. Jerome Emiliani
- ☐ St. John Baptist de la Salle
- ☐ St. John Eudes
- ☐ St. John Leonardi
- ☐ St. John of Capistrano
- ☐ St. John of God
- ☐ St. John of Kanty
- ☐ St. John the Baptist
- ☐ St. Joseph Calasanz

- ☐ St. Lawrence Ruiz
- ☐ St. Luke
- ☐ St. Margaret Mary Alacoque
- ☐ St. Mark
- ☐ St. Martha
- ☐ St. Mary Magdalene
- ☐ St. Norbert
- ☐ St. Paul
- ☐ St. Paul of the Cross
- ☐ St. Peter Claver
- ☐ St. Peter Julian Eymard
- ☐ St. Philip Neri
- ☐ St. Raymond of Penafort
- ☐ St. Rita of Cascia
- ☐ St. Romuald
- ☐ St. Rose Philippine Duchesne
- ☐ St. Scholastica
- ☐ St. Sharbel Makhluf
- ☐ St. Stanislaus
- ☐ St. Teresa Benedicta of the Cross
- ☐ St. Timothy
- ☐ St. Titus
- ☐ St. Toribio de Mongrovejo
- ☐ St. Vincent Ferrer
- ☐ St. Wenceslaus

LITANY OF THE SAINTS

- ☐ St. Agatha
- ☐ St. Agnes
- ☐ St. Anastasia
- ☐ St. Benedict
- ☐ St. Cecilia
- ☐ St. Clare
- ☐ St. Cosmos
- ☐ St. Damian
- ☐ St. Dominic
- ☐ St. Lucy
- ☐ St. Martin
- ☐ St. Nicholas
- ☐ St. Sebastian
- ☐ St. Stephen
- ☐ St. Vincent

POPULAR SAINTS

- ☐ St. Angela Merici
- ☐ St. Bernadette
- ☐ St. Christopher
- ☐ St. Dymphna
- ☐ St. Faustina
- ☐ St. Francis of Assisi
- ☐ St. Gerard Majella
- ☐ St. Joan of Arc
- ☐ St. John Bosco
- ☐ St. John Neumann
- ☐ St. John Vianney
- ☐ St. Juan Diego
- ☐ St. Katharine Drexel
- ☐ St. Louis de Montfort
- ☐ St. Martin de Porres
- ☐ St. Padre Pio
- ☐ St. Patrick
- ☐ St. Rose of Lima
- ☐ St. Thomas More
- ☐ St. Valentine
- ☐ St. Veronica

PATRON SAINTS OF HOLY SOULS IN PURGATORY

- ☐ St. Gertrude
- ☐ St. John Macias
- ☐ St. Nicholas of Tolentino
- ☐ St. Odilo

PATRON SAINTS AGAINST EVIL SPIRITS

- ☐ St. Agrippina
- ☐ St. Amabilis of Auvergne
- ☐ St. Andrew Avillino
- ☐ St. Bruno
- ☐ St. Cyriacus
- ☐ St. Demetrius of Sermium
- ☐ St. Deodatus of Nevers
- ☐ St. Josephat Kunsevich
- ☐ St. Lucian
- ☐ St. Lucy Bufalari
- ☐ St. Marcian
- ☐ St. Margaret of Antioch

- ☐ St. Margaret of Fontana
- ☐ St. Patroclus of Troyes
- ☐ St. Paulinus of Nola
- ☐ St. Quirinus
- ☐ St. Ubaldus Baldessini

INCORRUPTIBLES

- ☐ St. Charbel Makhlouf
- ☐ St. Josaphat
- ☐ St. Mary Magdalene de Pazzi
- ☐ St. Veronica Giulani
- ☐ St. Vincent de Paul
- ☐ St. Zita

MARTYRS

- ☐ St. Andrew Kim Taegon
- ☐ St. Blaise
- ☐ St. Charles Lwanga
- ☐ St. Claudius the Martyr
- ☐ St. Denis
- ☐ St. Dionysia the Martyr
- ☐ St. Felicity
- ☐ St. Fidelis of Sigmaringen
- ☐ St. Hilaria the Martyr
- ☐ St. Hippolytus of Rome
- ☐ St. Januarius
- ☐ St. Jason the Martyr
- ☐ St. Jean de Brebeuf
- ☐ St. John Fisher
- ☐ St. Lawrence of Rome
- ☐ St. Maria Goretti
- ☐ St. Maurus the Martyr
- ☐ St. Maximilian Kolbe
- ☐ St. Pancras
- ☐ St. Paul Chong Hasang
- ☐ St. Paul Miki
- ☐ St. Perpetua
- ☐ St. Peter Chanel
- ☐ St. Peter the Exorcist
- ☐ St. Polycarp
- ☐ St. Stanislaus
- ☐ St. Thomas Becket

SAINTS WHO WERE POPES

- St. Linus
- St. Anacletus
- St. Clement I
- St. Evaristus
- St. Alexander I
- St. Sixtus I
- St. Telesphorus
- St. Hyginus
- St. Pius I
- St. Anicetus
- St. Soter
- St. Eleutherius
- St. Victor I
- St. Zephyrinus
- St. Callistus I
- St. Urban I
- St. Pontain
- St. Anterus
- St. Fabian
- St. Cornelius
- St. Lucius I
- St. Stephen I
- St. Sixtus II
- St. Dionysius
- St. Felix I
- St. Eutychian
- St. Gaius
- St. Marcellinus
- St. Marcellus I
- St. Eusebius
- St. Miltiades
- St. Sylvester I
- St. Marcus
- St. Julius I
- St. Damasus I
- St. Siricius
- St. Anastasius I
- St. Innocent I
- St. Zosimus
- St. Boniface I
- St. Celestine I
- St. Sixtus III
- St. Hilarius
- St. Simplicius
- St. Felix III
- St. Gelasius I
- St. Anastasius II
- St. Symmachus
- St. Hormisdas
- St. John I
- St. Felix IV
- St. Agapetus I
- St. Silverius
- St. Boniface IV
- St. Deusdedit
- St. Martin I
- St. Eugene I
- St. Vitalian
- St. Agatho
- St. Leo II
- St. Benedict II
- St. Sergius I
- St. Gregory II
- St. Gregory III
- St. Zachary
- St. Paul I
- St. Leo III
- St. Paschal I
- St. Leo IV
- St. Nicholas I the Great
- St. Adrian III
- St. Leo IX
- St. Gregory VII
- St. Celestine V
- St. Pius V
- St. Pius X

SAINTS WHO WERE FATHERS

- ☐ St. Adauctus
- ☐ St. Alonso Rodriguez
- ☐ St. Andrew of Arezzo
- ☐ St. Ansfrid of Utrecht
- ☐ St. Arnulf of Metz
- ☐ St. Artemius of Rome
- ☐ St. Catervus
- ☐ St. Dagobert II
- ☐ St. Donivald
- ☐ St. Edgar the Peaceful
- ☐ St. Edwin of Northumbria
- ☐ St. Ethelbert of Kent
- ☐ St. Eucherius of Lyon
- ☐ St. Eustachius
- ☐ St. Fiace
- ☐ St. Fragan
- ☐ St. Francis Borgia
- ☐ St. Gabinus
- ☐ St. Gregory of Langres
- ☐ St. Gregory the Illuminator
- ☐ St. Hubert of Liege
- ☐ St. Isidore the Farmer
- ☐ St. John the Almoner
- ☐ St. Leopold III
- ☐ St. Louis IX
- ☐ St. Michael Kozaki
- ☐ St. Nicholas of Flüe
- ☐ St. Nilus the Elder
- ☐ St. Nilus the Younger
- ☐ St. Orentius of Loret
- ☐ St. Pacian of Barcelona
- ☐ St. Palmatius of Rome
- ☐ St. Pepin of Landen
- ☐ St. Peter Lieou
- ☐ St. Peter Orseolo
- ☐ St. Philip of Rome
- ☐ St. Pinian
- ☐ St. Quirinus the Jailer
- ☐ St. Simplicius of Bourges
- ☐ St. Solomon I
- ☐ St. Stephen of Hungary
- ☐ St. Vincent Madelgaire
- ☐ St. Vitalis of Milan
- ☐ St. Vladimir I of Kiev
- ☐ St. Walbert of Hainault
- ☐ St. Walfrid

SAINTS WHO WERE MOTHERS

- ☐ St. Agia
- ☐ St. Amalburga
- ☐ St. Amunia
- ☐ St. Bathilde
- ☐ St. Bridget of Sweden
- ☐ St. Candida of Rome
- ☐ St. Cecilia Yu Sosa
- ☐ St. Clotilde
- ☐ St. Crispina
- ☐ St. Elizabeth
- ☐ St. Elizabeth Ann Seton
- ☐ St. Felicity of Rome
- ☐ St. Frances of Rome
- ☐ St. Gianna Beretta Molla
- ☐ St. Gladys
- ☐ St. Gorgonia
- ☐ St. Gwen
- ☐ St. Hedwig of Andechs
- ☐ St. Helena
- ☐ St. Hildegund
- ☐ St. Humility
- ☐ St. Ida of Herzfeld
- ☐ St. Jacoba
- ☐ St. Jeanne de Chantal
- ☐ St. Judith of Prussia
- ☐ St. Ludmila
- ☐ St. Margaret of Cortona
- ☐ St. Margaret of Scotland
- ☐ St. Monica
- ☐ St. Natalia
- ☐ St. Non
- ☐ St. Nonna
- ☐ St. Olga of Kiev
- ☐ St. Patricia of Nicomedia
- ☐ St. Paula of Rome
- ☐ St. Priscilla of Rome
- ☐ St. Publia

- ❑ St. Rita of Cascia
- ❑ St. Saxburgh of Ely
- ❑ St. Sigrada
- ❑ St. Silvia of Rome
- ❑ St. Sophia
- ❑ St. Valeria of Milan
- ❑ St. Waltrude
- ❑ St. Wilfrida
- ❑ St. Zoe of Pamphylia

SAINTS WHO WERE CONVERTS

- ❑ St. Acestes
- ❑ St. Anne Line
- ❑ St. Audax
- ❑ St. Aurea
- ❑ St. Auxibius
- ❑ St. Barbara
- ❑ St. Camilla
- ❑ St. Craton
- ❑ St. Felicity of Carthage
- ❑ St. Gentian
- ❑ St. Gonzaga Gonza
- ❑ St. Henry Morse
- ❑ St. Irene
- ❑ St. James the Hermit
- ❑ St. John Ogilvie
- ❑ St. John Roberts
- ❑ St. Joseph Mukasa
- ❑ St. Joseph of Arimathea
- ❑ St. Josephine Bakhita
- ❑ St. Kieran
- ❑ St. Kizito
- ❑ St. Libert
- ❑ St. Martin of Tours
- ❑ St. Mathurin
- ❑ St. Mellon
- ❑ St. Odo the Good
- ❑ St. Olaf II
- ❑ St. Palatias
- ❑ St. Pancras of Rome
- ❑ St. Paulina of Rome
- ❑ St. Pelagia the Penitent
- ❑ St. Peter Ou

- ❑ St. Philip the Deacon
- ❑ St. Processus
- ❑ St. Ptolemy of Nepi
- ❑ St. Pudens of Rome
- ❑ St. Quentin
- ❑ St. Ralph Sherwin
- ❑ St. Regina
- ❑ St. Romanos the Melodist
- ❑ St. Romaric
- ❑ St. Romulus
- ❑ St. Sallustia
- ❑ St. Thamel
- ❑ St. Valeria of Limoges

OTHER SAINTS

- ❑ _____
- ❑ _____
- ❑ _____
- ❑ _____
- ❑ _____
- ❑ _____
- ❑ _____
- ❑ _____
- ❑ _____
- ❑ _____
- ❑ _____
- ❑ _____
- ❑ _____
- ❑ _____
- ❑ _____
- ❑ _____
- ❑ _____
- ❑ _____
- ❑ _____
- ❑ _____
- ❑ _____
- ❑ _____
- ❑ _____
- ❑ _____
- ❑ _____
- ❑ _____
- ❑ _____
- ❑ _____
- ❑ _____

HOLY SOULS IN PURGATORY FOR WHOM TO PRAY

HOLY SOULS
- [ ] _____
- [ ] _____
- [ ] _____
- [ ] _____
- [ ] _____
- [ ] _____
- [ ] _____
- [ ] _____
- [ ] _____
- [ ] _____
- [ ] _____
- [ ] _____
- [ ] _____
- [ ] _____
- [ ] _____
- [ ] _____
- [ ] _____
- [ ] _____
- [ ] _____
- [ ] _____
- [ ] _____
- [ ] _____
- [ ] _____
- [ ] _____
- [ ] _____
- [ ] _____
- [ ] _____
- [ ] _____
- [ ] _____
- [ ] _____
- [ ] _____
- [ ] _____
- [ ] _____
- [ ] _____
- [ ] _____

HOLY SOULS
- [ ] _____
- [ ] _____
- [ ] _____
- [ ] _____
- [ ] _____
- [ ] _____
- [ ] _____
- [ ] _____
- [ ] _____
- [ ] _____
- [ ] _____
- [ ] _____
- [ ] _____
- [ ] _____
- [ ] _____
- [ ] _____
- [ ] _____
- [ ] _____
- [ ] _____
- [ ] _____
- [ ] _____
- [ ] _____
- [ ] _____
- [ ] _____
- [ ] _____
- [ ] _____
- [ ] _____
- [ ] _____
- [ ] _____
- [ ] _____
- [ ] _____
- [ ] _____
- [ ] _____
- [ ] _____
- [ ] _____

HOLY SOULS

- ☐ _____
- ☐ _____
- ☐ _____
- ☐ _____
- ☐ _____
- ☐ _____
- ☐ _____
- ☐ _____
- ☐ _____
- ☐ _____
- ☐ _____
- ☐ _____
- ☐ _____
- ☐ _____
- ☐ _____
- ☐ _____
- ☐ _____
- ☐ _____
- ☐ _____
- ☐ _____
- ☐ _____
- ☐ _____
- ☐ _____
- ☐ _____
- ☐ _____
- ☐ _____
- ☐ _____
- ☐ _____
- ☐ _____
- ☐ _____
- ☐ _____
- ☐ _____
- ☐ _____
- ☐ _____
- ☐ _____
- ☐ _____
- ☐ _____
- ☐ _____
- ☐ _____
- ☐ _____
- ☐ _____

HOLY SOULS

- ☐ _____
- ☐ _____
- ☐ _____
- ☐ _____
- ☐ _____
- ☐ _____
- ☐ _____
- ☐ _____
- ☐ _____
- ☐ _____
- ☐ _____
- ☐ _____
- ☐ _____
- ☐ _____
- ☐ _____
- ☐ _____
- ☐ _____
- ☐ _____
- ☐ _____
- ☐ _____
- ☐ _____
- ☐ _____
- ☐ _____
- ☐ _____
- ☐ _____
- ☐ _____
- ☐ _____
- ☐ _____
- ☐ _____
- ☐ _____
- ☐ _____
- ☐ _____
- ☐ _____
- ☐ _____
- ☐ _____
- ☐ _____
- ☐ _____
- ☐ _____
- ☐ _____
- ☐ _____
- ☐ _____

JOURNAL TWO:
PRAYER REQUESTS

JOURNAL TWO: PRAYER REQUESTS

Pray for Others with Padre Pio Power!

"Prayer is the most potent force known to humanity. Because we have been made partakers in Jesus' victory over sin and death (1 Jn 4:4), we have the authority as sons and daughters of God to pray for others, pushing back the darkness of sin and oppression. In prayer, we have a weapon that has "divine power to destroy strongholds" (2 Cor 10:4). That kind of weaponry — the power of prayer — is something God invites us to use as we seek not only personal transformation but the transformation of the world as well. An intercessor is one who takes up a "burden" that goes far beyond his or her own needs and intentions."[69] — That is how *Partners in Evangelism* describes the immense power of prayer.

The Catechism of the Catholic Church teaches, "The first movement of the prayer of petition is *asking forgiveness,* like the tax collector in the parable: 'God, be merciful to me a sinner!' It is a prerequisite for righteous and pure prayer. A trusting humility brings us back into the light of communion between the Father and His Son Jesus Christ and with one another, so that 'we receive from Him whatever we ask' (1 Jn 3:22). Asking forgiveness is the prerequisite for both the Eucharistic liturgy and personal prayer" (CCC 2631).

When someone asks you to pray for them, why not pray with "Padre Pio Power"? When I heard that the prayer below (written by St. Margaret Mary Alacoque) was the one Padre Pio would use when people asked him to pray for them, I needed no further encouragement for choosing this prayer in the same way. Padre Pio has tens of thousands of miracles associated with him, including the healing of a very good friend of Pope John Paul II.

A convenient journal section has been created to record these special intentions. Keep in mind this type of petition is for specific needs such as gainful employment or healing from an illness. After some time has passed, refer back to this journal to record the amazing way God answers these prayers. Due to our limited view and God's eternal view, it is important to always trust that He knows far better what is really needed in these situations. Be open to seeing how sometimes He answers our specific prayers in a way that does not always match exactly with what we asked. When looking back on these petitions, see how His way is better.

Padre Pio's Sacred Heart Novena Prayer

O my Jesus, You have said: "Truly I say to you, ask and you will receive, seek and you will find, knock and it will be opened to you." Behold I knock, I seek and ask for the grace of *(here name your request)*. Our Father ... Hail Mary ... Glory Be ... Sacred Heart of Jesus, I place all my trust in You.

O my Jesus, You have said: "Truly I say to you, if you ask anything of the Father in My name, He will give it to you." Behold, in Your name, I ask the Father for the grace of *(here name your request)*. Our Father ... Hail Mary ... Glory Be ... Sacred Heart of Jesus, I place all my trust in You.

O my Jesus, You have said: "Truly I say to you, heaven and earth will pass away but My words will not pass away." Encouraged by Your infallible words I now ask for the grace of *(here name your request)*. Our Father ... Hail Mary ... Glory Be ... Sacred Heart of Jesus, I place all my trust in You.

O Sacred Heart of Jesus, for whom it is impossible not to have compassion on the afflicted, have pity on us miserable sinners and grant us the grace which we ask of You, through the Sorrowful and Immaculate Heart of Mary, Your tender Mother and ours.

Say the Hail, Holy Queen (page 166) and add: "St. Joseph, foster father of Jesus, pray for us."

How to use the Prayer Requests Journal

1. Write the name of the person who is in need of a special prayer in the COMRADE IN NEED column.

2. Write your specific prayer request for them in the PRAYER REQUEST column. Keep in mind these intentions are generally more specific than a person's spiritual conversion. Pray the Sacred Heart Novena Prayer and place a checkmark next to PIO PRAYER.

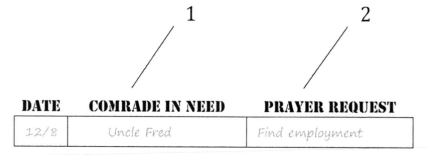

3. After some time has passed, write how God answered these prayers in the GLORY REPORT column. Always keep in mind that God knows best what is needed in a given situation to fulfill our ultimate goal of being with Him in heaven.

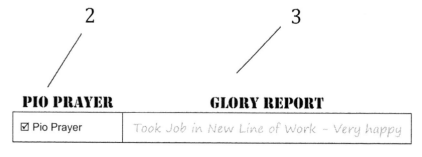

PRAYER REQUESTS JOURNAL

PRAYER REQUESTS

DATE	COMRADE IN NEED	PRAYER REQUEST

PRAYER REQUESTS

PIO PRAYER	GLORY REPORT
❑ Pio Prayer	
❑ Pio Prayer	
❑ Pio Prayer	
❑ Pio Prayer	
❑ Pio Prayer	
❑ Pio Prayer	
❑ Pio Prayer	
❑ Pio Prayer	
❑ Pio Prayer	
❑ Pio Prayer	
❑ Pio Prayer	
❑ Pio Prayer	
❑ Pio Prayer	
❑ Pio Prayer	
❑ Pio Prayer	
❑ Pio Prayer	
❑ Pio Prayer	
❑ Pio Prayer	
❑ Pio Prayer	
❑ Pio Prayer	
❑ Pio Prayer	

PRAYER REQUESTS

DATE	COMRADE IN NEED	PRAYER REQUEST

PRAYER REQUESTS

PIO PRAYER	GLORY REPORT
❑ Pio Prayer	
❑ Pio Prayer	
❑ Pio Prayer	
❑ Pio Prayer	
❑ Pio Prayer	
❑ Pio Prayer	
❑ Pio Prayer	
❑ Pio Prayer	
❑ Pio Prayer	
❑ Pio Prayer	
❑ Pio Prayer	
❑ Pio Prayer	
❑ Pio Prayer	
❑ Pio Prayer	
❑ Pio Prayer	
❑ Pio Prayer	
❑ Pio Prayer	
❑ Pio Prayer	
❑ Pio Prayer	
❑ Pio Prayer	
❑ Pio Prayer	

PRAYER REQUESTS

DATE	COMRADE IN NEED	PRAYER REQUEST

PRAYER REQUESTS

PIO PRAYER	GLORY REPORT
❑ Pio Prayer	
❑ Pio Prayer	
❑ Pio Prayer	
❑ Pio Prayer	
❑ Pio Prayer	
❑ Pio Prayer	
❑ Pio Prayer	
❑ Pio Prayer	
❑ Pio Prayer	
❑ Pio Prayer	
❑ Pio Prayer	
❑ Pio Prayer	
❑ Pio Prayer	
❑ Pio Prayer	
❑ Pio Prayer	
❑ Pio Prayer	
❑ Pio Prayer	
❑ Pio Prayer	
❑ Pio Prayer	
❑ Pio Prayer	
❑ Pio Prayer	

PART THREE:
CHURCH MILITANT BOOT CAMP

JOURNAL THREE:
CHURCH MILITANT BOOT CAMP

"You shall love the Lord your God with all your heart, and with all your soul, and with all your mind, and with all your strength." — Mark 12:30

"He must increase, but I must decrease" (Jn 3:30). St. John the Baptist knew his mission was not about himself but to prepare the way of the Lord. In the same way, we who are called to be warrior saints need to grow in our understanding that it is not about "me," it is about God and His mission of saving souls.

In the U.S. Army's Basic Combat Training, the first goal of the drill sergeants is to get everyone working and functioning as a team so they can accomplish the goals set before them. This is why one of the first phases of the training includes shaving all heads, as all recruits wear the same uniform. Why? Because there can be no elitism and no stereotypes if they are to work together as a team, a unified fighting force.

Real love — heroic love — is selfless; it is not egocentric, but absolutely self-emptying, as we identify in the supreme sacrifice of love in our crucified Lord and Savior, Jesus Christ. Similarly, the accounts of military bravery usually include a soldier's willingness to put himself in harm's way while he places the welfare of his comrades ahead of his own safety and security.

This is what St. Paul was getting at when he wrote: "I have been crucified with Christ; it is no longer I who live, but Christ who lives in me; and the life I now live in the flesh I live in the Son of God, Who loved me and gave Himself for me" (Gal 2:20). We Christians-in-training are forever looking for opportunities to empty ourselves in order to allow Christ to fill us.

This is why the Church Militant Boot Camp looks no further than the four facets of love Christ identified as the summation of the entire law and the prophets: "You shall love the Lord your God with all your heart, and with all your soul, and with all your mind, and with all your strength" (Mk 12:30). And then to understand that the second great commandment — "You shall love your neighbor as yourself" — is the natural consequence and result of the first, because a person who genuinely loves God also loves others because he knows we are all brothers and sisters, children of the same Father.

Heart

Love the Lord your God with all your heart: What is our first priority? Where does our heart lie? If we are consumed by thoughts of the next meeting or problem or bill, then our heart is in the wrong place. It takes great faith to trust Jesus who said, "Seek first the kingdom of God and His righteousness, and all these things will be given you besides" (Mt 6:33), yet He has remained faithful to those words time and time again.

To seek first the kingdom of God is to seek what matters most to God, and that is souls. To love God with all your heart means to strive to have the heart of God. It is a heart that burns for souls. From the Diary of St.

Faustina, our Lord tells us, "Zeal for the salvation of souls should burn in our hearts" (Diary 350).

Recall that you have been commissioned an officer in the Church Militant. This means that your love and concern is initiated through the powers of the offices we receive in Baptism: priest, prophet, and king. As we said, you will want to hone your skills for sharing with loved ones the hope that is within you (prophet), and you will want to cheerfully accept every opportunity and challenge to bravely demonstrate your resolve to place the kingdom of God first in your life (king). You'll want to be strong in God's grace and well prepared when situations such as these arise for you to deploy these actions.

But, intercessory prayer and sacrifice (priest) is something we can actually schedule into our daily lives, especially as we have learned that every day we are gifted with a chance to offer one plenary indulgence (and only one) for a deceased loved one. We also learned that we could then ask our amassing Holy Alliance to join us in prayer for a living soul to receive the supernatural grace of faith, hope, and love. Finally, every day can be a day to offer our prayers for those with other needs (health, work, etc.).

Recommendations: Follow the directions on page 85 for your daily mission of search and rescue for a holy soul in purgatory and a fellow comrade in the Church Militant you feel could use God's amazing breakthrough of grace. In the Prayers of Petition section starting on page 109, keep track of those you pray for who have other kinds of needs.

Soul

Love the Lord your God with all your soul: The Catechism of the Catholic Church teaches that while the human person, created in the image of God, is a being at once corporeal and spiritual, the "soul also refers to the innermost aspect of man, that which is of greatest value in him, that by which he is most especially in God's image: 'soul' signifies the *spiritual principle* in man" (CCC 363).

Pope John Paul II extended an invitation to all of us during the canonization of St. Josemaria Escriva: "'Put out into the deep,' the divine Teacher says to us, 'and let down your nets for a catch' (Lk 5:4). To fulfill such a rigorous mission, one needs constant interior growth nourished by prayer. St. Josemaria was a master in the practice of prayer, which he considered to be an extraordinary 'weapon' to redeem the world. He always recommended: 'In the first place prayer; then expiation; in the third place, but very much in third place, action' (*The Way*, n. 82). It is not a paradox but a perennial truth: the fruitfulness of the apostolate lies above all in prayer and in intense and constant sacramental life. This, in essence, is the secret of the holiness and the true success of the saints."[70]

Recommendations: Over the course of the 12-week boot camp, slowly incorporate the Seven Daily Habits for Holy Apostolic People as outlined on page 64. In two-week increments, add one or two of these habits.

Mind

Love the Lord your God with all your mind: All of us are in spiritual darkness, to some degree. Jesus comes as light and truth. When there is a breakthrough of grace, we see everything differently and we have different aspirations. The Divine Life transforms our natural propensity for wealth, pleasure, power, and honor. There is a breakthrough of a new world, God's life, and a new perspective breaks in. It is amazing to witness a soul who has received this incredible gift. At once, there is an unquenchable thirst to know God more.

We must pray for this amazing breakthrough of grace, but we must also position ourselves in the best place for receiving this gift. That is why this Church Militant Boot Camp has recruits begin by turning to some very powerful devotional books that ask us to reflect upon only a few sentences each day. By beginning with these bite-sized portions of spiritual reading, recruits will begin to notice their hearts being prepared for this breakthrough of grace.

Recommendations: I highly recommend starting your boot camp with the *Preparation for Total Consecration* by St. Louis de Montfort. This consecration to Jesus through Mary is a great way to call out to God for that breakthrough of grace. It has very short daily reflections over a 33-day period. Other powerful daily devotionals are *My Daily Bread* by Fr. Anthony Paone, the *Diary of St. Faustina,* and *The Imitation of Christ* by Thomas à Kempis.

Strength

In *Gaudium et Spes* of the Council of Vatican II we read, "Man, though made of body and soul, is a unity. Through his very bodily condition he sums up in himself the elements of the material world. Through him they are thus brought to their highest perfection and can raise their voice in praise freely given to the Creator. For this reason man may not despise his bodily life. Rather he is obliged to regard his body as good and to hold it in honor since God has created it and will raise it up on the last day."[71]

We have a tendency to disconnect the pieces of our life — work, exercise, prayer — but it is usually true that if we are flabby, our faith tends to be flabby. God has a real purpose for our lives, and it certainly is not true that God wills that it be hindered by frequent illnesses and fatigue.

Our "will" is that spiritual power of the soul by which we choose to do something. While fasting and abstinence are traditional forms of mortification of the flesh, why not add the challenge of a fitness regimen as an excellent way to, as we say in the Catholic world, "offer it up"? Certainly the discipline of diet and exercise will accomplish the goals of mortification, which is to die to the control worldly desires have over our lives. This is the true goal when we talk about "loving the Lord your God with all your strength."

Recommendation: *Body for Life* is outstanding for beginners or veterans. And, it lines up perfectly with this 12-week boot camp. You can order the book and journal online and/or use their website. Tony Horton's *Power 90 In-Home Boot Camp* is an excellent way to begin an exercise program. He follows up with *P90X*, for those who are a bit farther along. The South Beach Diet seems to have endured the test of time. I've also heard great things about *Light Weigh*, which incorporates a Catholic touch to it.

How to use the 12-Week Boot Camp Journal:

1. Write your goals for the week in these spaces under the appropriate category. Remember to start slowly and grow each week.

Heart: Search & Rescue — Prayer for a specific person or intention.

Soul: Interior Life — Specifics about your own prayer life.

Mind: Spiritual Reading — Grow in understanding of your faith.

Strength: Health & Fitness — Improve and maintain your body.

2. Schedule the time of day to fulfill your goals. Write each specific action in THE DAILY PLAN section.

1   2

HEART GOALS	SOUL GOALS
Divine Mercy Chaplet for Dad	*Morning Offering*
	Rosary
	Examination of Conscience

MIND GOALS	STRENGTH GOALS
Prep for Total Consecration	*Exercise 30 minutes*

THE DAILY PLAN			
5:00 AM		1:30 PM	
5:30 AM	*Morning Offering*	2:00 PM	
6:00 AM	*Exercise 30 minutes*	2:30 PM	
6:30 AM		3:00 PM	*Divine Mercy Chaplet*
7:00 AM		3:30 PM	

3. Record each day how closely you followed your plan by placing a check mark in the appropriate box for each activity you completed that day. The goal is to start slowly with attainable goals and work towards filling up the grid by the end of the 12-Week Boot Camp.

WEEK # 1	MON	TUE	WED	THU	FRI	SAT	SUN
HEART: SEARCH & RESCUE							
Soul in Purgatory - Indulgence							
Soul for Deeper Faith - DMC	✓	✓		✓	✓	✓	
Soul for Prayer - Pio Prayer							
SOUL: INTERIOR LIFE							
Morning Offering	✓	✓	✓	✓	✓	✓	✓
Mental Prayer							
Spiritual Reading							
Holy Mass							
Angelus (Regina Coeli)							
Holy Rosary		✓	✓		✓	✓	✓
Examination of Conscience	✓	✓	✓	✓	✓	✓	✓
MIND: SPIRITUAL READING							
Prep for Total Consecration	✓	✓	✓	✓		✓	
My Daily Bread							
Other:							
STRENGTH: HEALTH/FITNESS							
Daily Workout Goals		✓	✓	✓		✓	
Daily Dietary Goals							

12-WEEK CHURCH MILITANT BOOT CAMP JOURNAL

WEEKS 1 - 2 GOALS

"You shall love the Lord your God with all your heart, and with all your soul, and with all your mind, and with all your strength" (Mark 12:30).

HEART GOALS	SOUL GOALS

MIND GOALS	STRENGTH GOALS

THE DAILY PLAN

5:00 AM		1:30 PM	
5:30 AM		2:00 PM	
6:00 AM		2:30 PM	
6:30 AM		3:00 PM	
7:00 AM		3:30 PM	
7:30 AM		4:00 PM	
8:00 AM		4:30 PM	
8:30 AM		5:00 PM	
9:00 AM		5:30 PM	
9:30 AM		6:00 PM	
10:00 AM		6:30 PM	
10:30 AM		7:00 PM	
11:00 AM		7:30 PM	
11:30 AM		8:00 PM	
12:00 PM		8:30 PM	
12:30 PM		9:00 PM	
1:00 PM		9:30 PM	

WEEKS 1 – 2 PROGRESS

WEEK #__	MON	TUE	WED	THU	FRI	SAT	SUN
HEART: SEARCH & RESCUE							
Soul in Purgatory - Indulgence							
Soul for Deeper Faith - DMC							
Soul for Prayer - Pio Prayer							
SOUL: INTERIOR LIFE							
Morning Offering							
Mental Prayer							
Spiritual Reading							
Holy Mass							
Angelus (Regina Coeli)							
Holy Rosary							
Examination of Conscience							
MIND: SPIRITUAL READING							
Prep for Total Consecration							
My Daily Bread							
Other:							
STRENGTH: HEALTH/FITNESS							
Daily Workout Goals							
Daily Dietary Goals							

WEEK #__	MON	TUE	WED	THU	FRI	SAT	SUN
HEART: SEARCH & RESCUE							
Soul in Purgatory - Indulgence							
Soul for Deeper Faith - DMC							
Soul for Prayer - Pio Prayer							
SOUL: INTERIOR LIFE							
Morning Offering							
Mental Prayer							
Spiritual Reading							
Holy Mass							
Angelus (Regina Coeli)							
Holy Rosary							
Examination of Conscience							
MIND: SPIRITUAL READING							
Prep for Total Consecration							
My Daily Bread							
Other:							
STRENGTH: HEALTH/FITNESS							
Daily Workout Goals							
Daily Dietary Goals							

WEEKS 3 - 4 GOALS

"You shall love the Lord your God with all your heart, and with all your soul, and with all your mind, and with all your strength" (Mark 12:30).

HEART GOALS	SOUL GOALS

MIND GOALS	STRENGTH GOALS

THE DAILY PLAN			
5:00 AM		1:30 PM	
5:30 AM		2:00 PM	
6:00 AM		2:30 PM	
6:30 AM		3:00 PM	
7:00 AM		3:30 PM	
7:30 AM		4:00 PM	
8:00 AM		4:30 PM	
8:30 AM		5:00 PM	
9:00 AM		5:30 PM	
9:30 AM		6:00 PM	
10:00 AM		6:30 PM	
10:30 AM		7:00 PM	
11:00 AM		7:30 PM	
11:30 AM		8:00 PM	
12:00 PM		8:30 PM	
12:30 PM		9:00 PM	
1:00 PM		9:30 PM	

WEEKS 3 – 4 PROGRESS

WEEK #__	MON	TUE	WED	THU	FRI	SAT	SUN
HEART: SEARCH & RESCUE							
Soul in Purgatory - Indulgence							
Soul for Deeper Faith - DMC							
Soul for Prayer - Pio Prayer							
SOUL: INTERIOR LIFE							
Morning Offering							
Mental Prayer							
Spiritual Reading							
Holy Mass							
Angelus (Regina Coeli)							
Holy Rosary							
Examination of Conscience							
MIND: SPIRITUAL READING							
Prep for Total Consecration							
My Daily Bread							
Other:							
STRENGTH: HEALTH/FITNESS							
Daily Workout Goals							
Daily Dietary Goals							

WEEK #__	MON	TUE	WED	THU	FRI	SAT	SUN
HEART: SEARCH & RESCUE							
Soul in Purgatory - Indulgence							
Soul for Deeper Faith - DMC							
Soul for Prayer - Pio Prayer							
SOUL: INTERIOR LIFE							
Morning Offering							
Mental Prayer							
Spiritual Reading							
Holy Mass							
Angelus (Regina Coeli)							
Holy Rosary							
Examination of Conscience							
MIND: SPIRITUAL READING							
Prep for Total Consecration							
My Daily Bread							
Other:							
STRENGTH: HEALTH/FITNESS							
Daily Workout Goals							
Daily Dietary Goals							

WEEKS 5 - 6 GOALS

"You shall love the Lord your God with all your heart, and with all your soul, and with all your mind, and with all your strength" (Mark 12:30).

HEART GOALS	SOUL GOALS

MIND GOALS	STRENGTH GOALS

THE DAILY PLAN

5:00 AM		1:30 PM	
5:30 AM		2:00 PM	
6:00 AM		2:30 PM	
6:30 AM		3:00 PM	
7:00 AM		3:30 PM	
7:30 AM		4:00 PM	
8:00 AM		4:30 PM	
8:30 AM		5:00 PM	
9:00 AM		5:30 PM	
9:30 AM		6:00 PM	
10:00 AM		6:30 PM	
10:30 AM		7:00 PM	
11:00 AM		7:30 PM	
11:30 AM		8:00 PM	
12:00 PM		8:30 PM	
12:30 PM		9:00 PM	
1:00 PM		9:30 PM	

WEEKS 5 – 6 PROGRESS

WEEK #__	MON	TUE	WED	THU	FRI	SAT	SUN
HEART: SEARCH & RESCUE							
Soul in Purgatory - Indulgence							
Soul for Deeper Faith - DMC							
Soul for Prayer - Pio Prayer							
SOUL: INTERIOR LIFE							
Morning Offering							
Mental Prayer							
Spiritual Reading							
Holy Mass							
Angelus (Regina Coeli)							
Holy Rosary							
Examination of Conscience							
MIND: SPIRITUAL READING							
Prep for Total Consecration							
My Daily Bread							
Other:							
STRENGTH: HEALTH/FITNESS							
Daily Workout Goals							
Daily Dietary Goals							

WEEK #__	MON	TUE	WED	THU	FRI	SAT	SUN
HEART: SEARCH & RESCUE							
Soul in Purgatory - Indulgence							
Soul for Deeper Faith - DMC							
Soul for Prayer - Pio Prayer							
SOUL: INTERIOR LIFE							
Morning Offering							
Mental Prayer							
Spiritual Reading							
Holy Mass							
Angelus (Regina Coeli)							
Holy Rosary							
Examination of Conscience							
MIND: SPIRITUAL READING							
Prep for Total Consecration							
My Daily Bread							
Other:							
STRENGTH: HEALTH/FITNESS							
Daily Workout Goals							
Daily Dietary Goals							

WEEKS 7 - 8 GOALS

"You shall love the Lord your God with all your heart, and with all your soul, and with all your mind, and with all your strength" (Mark 12:30).

HEART GOALS	SOUL GOALS

MIND GOALS	STRENGTH GOALS

THE DAILY PLAN			
5:00 AM		1:30 PM	
5:30 AM		2:00 PM	
6:00 AM		2:30 PM	
6:30 AM		3:00 PM	
7:00 AM		3:30 PM	
7:30 AM		4:00 PM	
8:00 AM		4:30 PM	
8:30 AM		5:00 PM	
9:00 AM		5:30 PM	
9:30 AM		6:00 PM	
10:00 AM		6:30 PM	
10:30 AM		7:00 PM	
11:00 AM		7:30 PM	
11:30 AM		8:00 PM	
12:00 PM		8:30 PM	
12:30 PM		9:00 PM	
1:00 PM		9:30 PM	

WEEKS 7 – 8 PROGRESS

WEEK #__	MON	TUE	WED	THU	FRI	SAT	SUN
HEART: SEARCH & RESCUE							
Soul in Purgatory - Indulgence							
Soul for Deeper Faith - DMC							
Soul for Prayer - Pio Prayer							
SOUL: INTERIOR LIFE							
Morning Offering							
Mental Prayer							
Spiritual Reading							
Holy Mass							
Angelus (Regina Coeli)							
Holy Rosary							
Examination of Conscience							
MIND: SPIRITUAL READING							
Prep for Total Consecration							
My Daily Bread							
Other:							
STRENGTH: HEALTH/FITNESS							
Daily Workout Goals							
Daily Dietary Goals							

WEEK #__	MON	TUE	WED	THU	FRI	SAT	SUN
HEART: SEARCH & RESCUE							
Soul in Purgatory - Indulgence							
Soul for Deeper Faith - DMC							
Soul for Prayer - Pio Prayer							
SOUL: INTERIOR LIFE							
Morning Offering							
Mental Prayer							
Spiritual Reading							
Holy Mass							
Angelus (Regina Coeli)							
Holy Rosary							
Examination of Conscience							
MIND: SPIRITUAL READING							
Prep for Total Consecration							
My Daily Bread							
Other:							
STRENGTH: HEALTH/FITNESS							
Daily Workout Goals							
Daily Dietary Goals							

WEEKS 9 - 10 GOALS

"You shall love the Lord your God with all your heart, and with all your soul, and with all your mind, and with all your strength" (Mark 12:30).

HEART GOALS	SOUL GOALS

MIND GOALS	STRENGTH GOALS

THE DAILY PLAN			
5:00 AM		1:30 PM	
5:30 AM		2:00 PM	
6:00 AM		2:30 PM	
6:30 AM		3:00 PM	
7:00 AM		3:30 PM	
7:30 AM		4:00 PM	
8:00 AM		4:30 PM	
8:30 AM		5:00 PM	
9:00 AM		5:30 PM	
9:30 AM		6:00 PM	
10:00 AM		6:30 PM	
10:30 AM		7:00 PM	
11:00 AM		7:30 PM	
11:30 AM		8:00 PM	
12:00 PM		8:30 PM	
12:30 PM		9:00 PM	
1:00 PM		9:30 PM	

WEEKS 9 – 10 PROGRESS

WEEK #__	MON	TUE	WED	THU	FRI	SAT	SUN
HEART: SEARCH & RESCUE							
Soul in Purgatory - Indulgence							
Soul for Deeper Faith - DMC							
Soul for Prayer - Pio Prayer							
SOUL: INTERIOR LIFE							
Morning Offering							
Mental Prayer							
Spiritual Reading							
Holy Mass							
Angelus (Regina Coeli)							
Holy Rosary							
Examination of Conscience							
MIND: SPIRITUAL READING							
Prep for Total Consecration							
My Daily Bread							
Other:							
STRENGTH: HEALTH/FITNESS							
Daily Workout Goals							
Daily Dietary Goals							

WEEK #__	MON	TUE	WED	THU	FRI	SAT	SUN
HEART: SEARCH & RESCUE							
Soul in Purgatory - Indulgence							
Soul for Deeper Faith - DMC							
Soul for Prayer - Pio Prayer							
SOUL: INTERIOR LIFE							
Morning Offering							
Mental Prayer							
Spiritual Reading							
Holy Mass							
Angelus (Regina Coeli)							
Holy Rosary							
Examination of Conscience							
MIND: SPIRITUAL READING							
Prep for Total Consecration							
My Daily Bread							
Other:							
STRENGTH: HEALTH/FITNESS							
Daily Workout Goals							
Daily Dietary Goals							

WEEKS 11 - 12 GOALS

"You shall love the Lord your God with all your heart, and with all your soul, and with all your mind, and with all your strength" (Mark 12:30).

HEART GOALS	SOUL GOALS

MIND GOALS	STRENGTH GOALS

THE DAILY PLAN

5:00 AM		1:30 PM	
5:30 AM		2:00 PM	
6:00 AM		2:30 PM	
6:30 AM		3:00 PM	
7:00 AM		3:30 PM	
7:30 AM		4:00 PM	
8:00 AM		4:30 PM	
8:30 AM		5:00 PM	
9:00 AM		5:30 PM	
9:30 AM		6:00 PM	
10:00 AM		6:30 PM	
10:30 AM		7:00 PM	
11:00 AM		7:30 PM	
11:30 AM		8:00 PM	
12:00 PM		8:30 PM	
12:30 PM		9:00 PM	
1:00 PM		9:30 PM	

WEEKS 11 – 12 PROGRESS

WEEK #__	MON	TUE	WED	THU	FRI	SAT	SUN
HEART: SEARCH & RESCUE							
Soul in Purgatory - Indulgence							
Soul for Deeper Faith - DMC							
Soul for Prayer - Pio Prayer							
SOUL: INTERIOR LIFE							
Morning Offering							
Mental Prayer							
Spiritual Reading							
Holy Mass							
Angelus (Regina Coeli)							
Holy Rosary							
Examination of Conscience							
MIND: SPIRITUAL READING							
Prep for Total Consecration							
My Daily Bread							
Other:							
STRENGTH: HEALTH/FITNESS							
Daily Workout Goals							
Daily Dietary Goals							

WEEK #__	MON	TUE	WED	THU	FRI	SAT	SUN
HEART: SEARCH & RESCUE							
Soul in Purgatory - Indulgence							
Soul for Deeper Faith - DMC							
Soul for Prayer - Pio Prayer							
SOUL: INTERIOR LIFE							
Morning Offering							
Mental Prayer							
Spiritual Reading							
Holy Mass							
Angelus (Regina Coeli)							
Holy Rosary							
Examination of Conscience							
MIND: SPIRITUAL READING							
Prep for Total Consecration							
My Daily Bread							
Other:							
STRENGTH: HEALTH/FITNESS							
Daily Workout Goals							
Daily Dietary Goals							

APPENDIX ONE:
DAILY PRAYERS & PRACTICES

APPENDIX ONE: DAILY PRAYERS AND PRACTICES

Daytime Prayers

Morning Offering

O my God, in union with the Immaculate Heart of Mary (if applicable, here kiss your scapular as sign of your consecration to Mary), I offer Thee the Precious Blood of Jesus from all the altars throughout the world, joining with It the offering of my every thought, word, and action of this day. O my Jesus, I desire today to gain every indulgence and merit I can and I offer them, together with myself, to Mary Immaculate, that she may best apply them in the interests of Thy Most Sacred Heart. Precious Blood of Jesus, save us! Immaculate Heart of Mary, pray for us! Sacred Heart of Jesus, have mercy on us! (Conclude by praying for the pope's intentions; an Our Father and Hail Mary, or other appropriate prayer, is sufficient.)

The Angelus

V. The Angel of the Lord declared unto Mary,
R. And she conceived of the Holy Spirit.
Hail Mary ...
V. Behold the handmaid of the Lord,
R. Be it done unto me according to thy word.
Hail Mary ...
V. And the Word was made Flesh,
R. And dwelt among us.
Hail Mary ...
V. Pray for us, O Holy Mother of God,
R. That we may be made worthy of the promises of Christ.
V. Let us pray. Pour forth, we beseech Thee, O Lord, Thy grace into our hearts; that we to whom the incarnation of Christ, Thy Son, was made known by the message of an angel, may, by His passion and cross, be brought to the glory of His resurrection. Through the same Christ our Lord.
All. Amen.

The Regina Coeli

Queen of Heaven rejoice, alleluia:
For He Whom you did merit to bear, alleluia,
Has risen as He said, alleluia.
Pray for us to God, alleluia.
Rejoice and be glad, O Virgin Mary, alleluia.
For the Lord has truly risen, alleluia.

Let us pray: O God, Who gave joy to the world through the resurrection of Thy Son, our Lord Jesus Christ, grant we beseech Thee, that through the intercession of the Virgin Mary, His mother, we may obtain the joys of everlasting life. Through the same Christ our Lord. Amen.

Mental Prayer

"Mental prayer is the blessed furnace in which souls are inflamed with the love of God. All the saints have become saints by mental prayer." — St. Alphonsus Ligouri

Mental prayer is a form of prayer recommended in the Catholic Church whereby one loves God through dialogue, meditating on God's words, and the contemplation of His Face. It is a time of silence focused on God.

"What matters in prayer is not what we do but what God does in us during those moments," said Fr. Jacques Philippe, "The essential act in prayer is, at bottom, to place one's self in God's presence and to remain there … This presence, which is that of the living God, is active, vivifying. It heals and sanctifies us. We cannot sit before a fire without getting warm."[72]

Preparatory Prayer: My Lord and my God, I firmly believe that You are here, that You see me, that You hear me. I adore You with profound reverence; I ask Your pardon for my sins, and the grace to make this time of prayer fruitful. My immaculate Mother, St. Joseph my father and lord, my guardian angel, intercede for me.

Heart Speaks to Heart (*Cor ad Cor Loquitor*): St. Josemaria Escriva described prayer thus: "To pray is to talk with God. But about what? … About Him, about yourself — joys, sorrows, successes and failures, noble ambitions, daily worries, weaknesses. And acts of thanksgiving and petitions and love and reparation. In a word, to get to know Him and to get to know yourself. To get acquainted!"[73]

Closing prayer: I thank You, my God, for the good resolutions, affections, and inspirations that You have communicated to me in this meditation. I ask Your help to put them into effect. My immaculate Mother, St. Joseph my father and lord, my guardian angel, intercede for me.

Lectio Divina (Divine Reading)

The following explanation of Lectio Divina is reprinted from Fisheaters.com.[74]

Read/Lectio: When we are relaxed and in a contemplative mode, we trace the Sign of the Cross on the book of Scripture, kiss the Cross we traced, and then open it to read. Some may want to focus on Scripture from the daily Mass. We aren't trying to "accomplish a goal" of reading X amount; we read what is easily digested at that time. Whichever selection we choose, we read it with our minds, slowly, gently, coming to an understanding of the words themselves.

Having a solid Catholic commentary helps us approach Scripture with the mind of the Church. We should always keep in mind Peter's admonition that "no prophecy of Scripture is made by private interpretation" (2 Pt 1:20) and that Scripture can be difficult to understand, something "which the unlearned and unstable wrest ... to their own destruction" (2 Pt 3:16).

Meditate/Meditatio: Now we meditate on what we have read, perhaps even reading it again, visualizing it, and listening for the aspect of it that reveals the Divine Mysteries. We want the deeper, spiritual meanings of the words now, in order to understand the deeper reality the Holy Spirit intends to convey by arranging nature and history as He did, thereby inspiring the writer of the text to write as he did.

Prayer/Oratio: We ask God for the grace to be changed by what we have read, to come more fully into being what He wants us to be, and to help us apply the moral sense of the Scripture to our lives.

Contemplation/Contemplatio: We rest in gratitude for God and His Word.

Evening Prayers

The following is outlined in the Handbook of Prayers, *edited by Fr. James Socias, as a good set of practices to follow for evening prayer.*[75]

Make a brief examination of conscience before going to bed at night. Two or three minutes will suffice.

Place yourself in the presence of God, recognizing His strength and your weakness. Tell Him: "Lord, if You will, You can make me clean."

Ask your guardian angel for light to acknowledge your defects and virtues: What have I done wrong? What have I done right? What could I have done better?

Examine your conscience with sincerity:

Did I often consider that God is my Father? Did I offer Him my work? Did I make good use of my time? Did I pray slowly and with attention? Did I try to make life pleasant for other people? Did I criticize anyone? Was I forgiving? Did I pray and offer some sacrifices for the Church, for the pope, and for those around me? Did I allow myself to be carried away by sensuality? By pride?

Make an Act of Contrition: O my God, I am heartily sorry for having offended Thee and I detest all my sins because I dread the loss of heaven and the pains of hell, but most of all because they offend Thee, my God, Who art all good and deserving of all my love. I firmly resolve, with the help of Thy grace, to sin no more and avoid the near occasions of sin. Amen.

Make a specific resolution for tomorrow: To stay away from certain temptations. To avoid some specific faults. To exert special effort to practice some virtue. To take advantage of occasion for improvement.

Pray three Hail Marys to the Virgin Mary, asking for purity of heart and body.

Manner of Making Confession

(Having entered the confessional, place yourself in the presence of God, Who sees all things, and then address His minister):

Bless me, Father, for I have sinned,

I confess to almighty God, and to you, Father, that I have sinned exceedingly in thought, word, deed, and omission, through my fault.

It has been ___ weeks since my last Confession. I accuse myself of having committed, during that time, the following sins:

(State your sins here)

For these, and all the sins of which I have at any time been guilty, I humbly ask pardon of God, and absolution of you, Father, if you think me worthy.

(Then listen intently to anything the confessor may choose to say; humbly accept the penance he imposes, and, once he has completed the prayer of absolution, recite the act of contrition.)

The Act of Contrition: O My God, I am heartily sorry for having offended Thee and I detest all my sins because I dread the loss of heaven and the pains of hell, but most of all because they offend Thee, my God, Who art all good and deserving of all my love. I firmly resolve, with the help of Thy grace, to sin no more and avoid the near occasions of sin. Amen.

(After Confession we should return thanks to God for His mercies in forgiving our sins, beg that He supply whatever has been wanting in us and bless our good resolutions, and immediately thereafter say our penance.)

Examination of Conscience

Special thanks to Beginning Catholic *for this examination.*[76]

We use an examination of conscience to help call to mind our sins and failings during a period of quiet reflection before approaching the priest in Confession. It's important for a good Catholic examination of conscience to be thorough. This will help you learn about things that you may not be aware of. It's also a chance to develop your conscience.

To make an examination:

✠ Set aside some quiet time for reflection.

✠ Start by praying to the Holy Spirit, asking for help in making a good examination to prepare for Confession.

✠ Read through the items on this list and honestly reflect on your behavior for each item.

✠ If necessary, take this list or brief notes (keep them private!) to Confession to help you remember things.

First Commandment:

You shall worship the Lord your God and Him only shall you serve. Have I ...

✠ Disobeyed the commandments of God or the Church?

✠ Refused to accept what God has revealed as true, or what the Catholic Church proposes for belief?

✠ Denied the existence of God?

✠ Failed to nourish and protect my faith?

✠ Rejected everything opposed to a sound faith?

✠ Deliberately misled others about doctrine or the faith?

✠ Rejected the Catholic faith, joined another Christian denomination, or joined or practiced another religion?

✠ Joined a group forbidden to Catholics (Masons, communists, etc.)?

✠ Despaired about my salvation or the forgiveness of my sins?

✠ Presumed on God's mercy? (Committing a sin in expectation of forgiveness, or asking for forgiveness without conversion and practicing virtue.)

✠ Loved someone or something more than God (money, power, sex, ambition, etc.)?

✠ Let someone or something influence my choices more than God?

✠ Engaged in superstitious practices? (Including horoscopes, fortunetellers, etc.)

✠ Been involved in the occult? (séances, Ouija board, worship of Satan, etc.)

✠ Formally left the Catholic Church?

✠ Hidden a serious sin or told a lie in Confession?

Second Commandment

You shall not take the name of the Lord your God in vain. Have I...

✠ Used the name of God in cursing or blasphemy?

✠ Failed to keep vows or promises that I have made to God?

✠ Spoken about the faith, the Church, the saints, or sacred things with irreverence, hatred, or defiance?

✠ Watched television or movies or listened to music that treated God, the Church, the saints, or sacred things irreverently?

✠ Used vulgar, suggestive, or obscene speech?

✠ Belittled others in my speech?

✠ Behaved disrespectfully in Church?

✠ Misused places or things set apart for the worship of God?

✠ Committed perjury? (Breaking an oath or lying under oath.)

✠ Blamed God for my failings?

Third Commandment

Remember to keep holy the Sabbath day. Have I ...

✠ Set time aside each day for personal prayer to God?

✠ Missed Mass on Sunday or Holy Days (through my own fault without sufficient reason)?

✠ Committed a sacrilege against the Blessed Sacrament?

✠ Received a sacrament while in the state of mortal sin?

✠ Habitually came late to and/or left early from Mass without a good reason?

✠ Shopped, labored, or done business unnecessarily on Sunday or other Holy Days of Obligation?

✠ Not attended to taking my children to Mass?

✠ Knowingly eaten meat on a day of abstinence (or not fasted on a fast day)?

✠ Eaten or drank within one hour of receiving Communion (other than water or medical need)?

Fourth Commandment

Honor your father and your mother. Have I ...

✠ Obeyed all that my parents reasonably asked of me? (If still under my parents' care.)

✠ Neglected the needs of my parents in their old age or in their time of need?

✠ Obeyed the reasonable demands of my teachers? (If still in school.)

✠ Neglected to give my children proper food, clothing, shelter, education, discipline, and care (even after Confirmation)?

✠ Provided for the religious education and formation of my children for as long as they were under my care?

✠ Ensured that my children still under my care regularly frequent the sacraments of Penance and Holy Communion?

✠ Educated my children in a way that corresponds to my religious convictions?

✠ Provided my children with a positive, prudent, and personalized education in the Catholic teaching on human sexuality?

✠ Been to my children a good example of how to live the Catholic faith?

✠ Prayed with and for my children?

✠ Lived in humble obedience to those who legitimately exercise authority over me?

✠ Broken the law?

✠ Supported or voted for a politician whose positions are opposed to the teachings of Christ and the Catholic Church?

Fifth Commandment

You shall not kill. Have I ...

✠ Unjustly and intentionally killed a human being?

✠ Been involved in an abortion, directly or indirectly (through advice, etc.)?

✠ Seriously considered or attempted suicide?

✠ Supported, promoted, or encouraged the practice of assisted suicide or mercy killing?

✠ Deliberately desired to kill an innocent human being?

✠ Unjustly inflicted bodily harm on another person?

✠ Unjustly threatened another person with bodily harm?

✠ Verbally or emotionally abused another person?

✠ Hated another person, or wished him evil?

✠ Been prejudiced or unjustly discriminating against others because of their race, color, nationality, sex, or religion?

✠ Joined a hate group?

✠ Purposely provoked another by teasing or nagging?

✠ Recklessly endangered my life or health, or that of another, by my actions?

✠ Driven recklessly or under the influence of alcohol or other drugs?

✠ Abused alcohol or other drugs?

✠ Sold or given drugs to others to use for non-therapeutic purposes?

✠ Used tobacco immoderately?

✠ Over-eaten?

✠ Encouraged others to sin by giving scandal?

✠ Helped another to commit a mortal sin? (through advice, driving them somewhere, etc.)

✠ Caused serious injury or death by criminal neglect?

✠ Indulged in serious anger?

✠ Refused to control my temper?

✠ Been mean to, quarreled with, or willfully hurt someone?

✠ Been unforgiving to others, when mercy or pardon was requested?

✠ Sought revenge or hoped something bad would happen to someone?

✠ Delighted to see someone else get hurt or suffer?

✠ Treated animals cruelly, causing them to suffer or die needlessly?

Sixth and Ninth Commandments

You shall not commit adultery. You shall not covet your neighbor's wife. Have I ...

✠ Practiced the virtue of chastity?

✠ Given in to lust? (The desire for sexual pleasure unrelated to spousal love in marriage.)

✠ Used an artificial means of birth control?

✠ Refused to be open to conception, without just cause? (Catechism of the Catholic Church paragraph 2368)

✠ Participated in immoral techniques for in vitro fertilization or artificial insemination?

✠ Sterilized my sex organs for contraceptive purposes?

✠ Deprived my spouse of the marital right, without just cause?

✠ Claimed my own marital right without concern for my spouse?

✠ Deliberately caused climax outside of normal sexual intercourse? (Catechism of the Catholic Church paragraph 2366)

✠ Willfully entertained impure thoughts?

✠ Purchased, viewed, or made use of pornography?

✠ Watched movies and television that involved sex and nudity?

✠ Listened to music or jokes that were harmful to purity?

✠ Committed adultery? (Sexual relations with someone who is married, or with someone other than my spouse.)

✠ Committed incest? (Sexual relations with a relative or in-law.)

✠ Committed fornication? (Sexual relations with someone of the opposite sex when neither is married.)

✠ Engaged in homosexual activity? (Sexual activity with someone of the same sex.)

✠ Committed rape?

✠ Masturbated? (Deliberate stimulation of one's own sexual organs for sexual pleasure.)

✠ Engaged in sexual foreplay (petting) reserved for marriage?

✠ Preyed upon children or youth for my sexual pleasure?

✠ Engaged in unnatural sexual activities?

✠ Engaged in prostitution, or paid for the services of a prostitute?

✠ Seduced someone, or allowed myself to be seduced?

✠ Made uninvited and unwelcome sexual advances toward another?

✠ Purposely dressed immodestly?

Seventh and Tenth Commandments

You shall not steal. You shall not covet your neighbor's goods. Have I ...

✠ Stolen? (Take something that doesn't belong to me against the reasonable will of the owner.)
✠ Envied others on account of their possessions?
✠ Tried to live in a spirit of Gospel poverty and simplicity?
✠ Given generously to others in need?
✠ Considered that God has provided me with money so that I might use it to benefit others, as well as for my own legitimate needs?
✠ Freed myself from a consumer mentality?
✠ Practiced the works of mercy?
✠ Deliberately defaced, destroyed, or lost another's property?
✠ Cheated on a test, taxes, sports, games, or in business?
✠ Squandered money in compulsive gambling?
✠ Make a false claim to an insurance company?
✠ Paid my employees a living wage, or failed to give a full day's work for a full day's pay?
✠ Failed to honor my part of a contract?
✠ Failed to make good on a debt?
✠ Overcharged someone, especially to take advantage of another's hardship or ignorance?
✠ Misused natural resources?

Eighth Commandment

You shall not bear false witness against your neighbor. Have I ...

✠ Lied?

✠ Knowingly and willfully deceived another?

✠ Perjured myself under oath?

✠ Gossiped?

✠ Committed detraction? (Destroying a person's reputation by telling others about his faults for no good reason.)

✠ Committed slander or calumny? (Telling lies about another person in order to destroy his reputation.)

✠ Committed libel? (Writing lies about another person in order to destroy his reputation.)

✠ Been guilty of rash judgment? (Assuming the worst of another person based on circumstantial evidence.)

✠ Failed to make reparation for a lie I told, or for harm done to a person's reputation?

✠ Failed to speak out in defense of the Catholic Faith, the Church, or of another person?

✠ Betrayed another's confidence through speech?

APPENDIX TWO:
PRAYERS

APPENDIX TWO: PRAYERS

Collection of Prayers

Sign of the Cross

In the Name of the Father and of the Son and of the Holy Spirit. Amen.

In nomine Patris, et Filii, et Spiritus Sancti. Amen.

Lord's Prayer (Our Father)

Our Father, Who art in heaven, hallowed be Thy name. Thy kingdom come; Thy will be done on earth, as it is in heaven. Give us this day our daily bread, and forgive us our trespasses, as we forgive those who trespass against us. And lead us not into temptation, but deliver us from evil. Amen.

Pater noster, qui es in caelis, sanctificetur nomen tuum. Adveniat regnum tuum. Fiat voluntas tua, sicut in caelo et in terra. Panem nostrum quotidianum da nobis hodie, et dimitte nobis debita nostra sicut et nos dimittimus debitoribus nostris. Et ne nos inducas in tentationem, sed libera nos a malo. Amen.

Hail Mary

Hail Mary, full of grace; the Lord is with thee; blessed art thou among women, and blessed is the fruit of thy womb, Jesus. Holy Mary, Mother of God, pray for us sinners, now and at the hour of our death. Amen.

Ave Maria, gratia plena, Dominus tecum. Benedicta tu in mulieribus, et benedictus fructus ventris tui, Iesus. Sancta Maria, Mater Dei, ora pro nobis peccatoribus, nunc, et in hora mortis nostrae. Amen.

Glory Be

Glory be to the Father, and to the Son, and to the Holy Spirit. As it was in the beginning, is now, and will be forever. Amen.

Gloria Patri, et Filio, et Spiritui Sancto. Sicut erat in principio, et nunc, et semper, et in saecula saeculorum. Amen.

Apostles' Creed

I believe in God, the Father almighty, Creator of heaven and earth, and in Jesus Christ, His only Son, our Lord, Who was conceived by the Holy Spirit, born of the Virgin Mary, suffered under Pontius Pilate, was crucified, died, and was buried; He descended into hell; on the third day He rose again from the dead; He ascended into heaven, and is seated at the right hand of God the Father almighty; from there He will come to judge the living and the dead. I believe in the Holy Spirit, the holy catholic Church, the communion of saints, the forgiveness of sins, the resurrection of the body, and life everlasting. Amen.

Credo in Deum Patrem omnipotentem, Creatorem caeli et terrae. Et in Iesum Christum, Filium eius unicum, Dominum nostrum, qui conceptus est de Spiritu Sancto, natus ex Maria Virgine, passus sub Pontio Pilato, crucifixus, mortuus, et sepultus, descendit ad infernos, tertia die resurrexit a mortuis, ascendit ad caelos, sedet ad dexteram Dei Patris omnipotentis, inde venturus est iudicare vivos et mortuos. Credo in Spiritum Sanctum, sanctam Ecclesiam catholicam, sanctorum communionem, remissionem peccatorum, carnis resurrectionem, vitam aeternam. Amen.

Nicene Creed

I believe in one God, the Father almighty, maker of heaven and earth, of all things visible and invisible.

I believe in one Lord Jesus Christ, the Only Begotten Son of God, born of the Father before all ages. God from God, Light from Light, true God from true God, begotten, not made, consubstantial with the Father; through Him all things were made. For us men and for our salvation He came down from heaven, and by the Holy Spirit was incarnate of the Virgin Mary, and became man. For our sake He was crucified under Pontius Pilate, He suffered death and was buried, and rose again on the third day in accordance with the Scriptures. He ascended into heaven and is seated at the right hand of the Father. He will come again in glory to judge the living and the dead and His kingdom will have no end.

I believe in the Holy Spirit, the Lord, the giver of life, Who proceeds from the Father and the Son, Who with the Father and the Son is adored and glorified, Who has spoken through the prophets.

I believe in one, holy, catholic, and apostolic Church. I confess one baptism for the forgiveness of sins, and I look forward to the resurrection of the dead and the life of the world to come. Amen.

Fatima Prayer

O my Jesus, forgive us our sins; save us from the fires of hell. Lead all souls to heaven, especially those who are most in need of Your mercy.

Domine Iesu, dimitte nobis debita nostra, salva nos ab igne inferiori, perduc in caelum omnes animas, praesertim eas, quae misericordiae tuae maxime indigent.

Hail, Holy Queen

Hail, holy Queen, Mother of Mercy; our life, our sweetness, and our hope. To thee do we cry, poor banished children of Eve; to thee do we send up our sighs, mourning and weeping in this valley of tears. Turn, then, most gracious advocate, thine eyes of mercy towards us; and after this our exile, show unto us the blessed fruit of thy womb, Jesus. O clement, O loving, O sweet Virgin Mary.

V. Pray for us, O holy Mother of God.

R. That we may be made worthy of the promises of Christ.

Salve Regina, Mater misericordiae. Vita, dulcedo, et spes nostra, salve. Ad te clamamus exsules filii Hevae. Ad te Suspiramus, gementes et flentes in hac lacrimarum valle. Eia ergo, Advocata nostra, illos tuos misericordes oculos ad nos converte. Et Iesum, benedictum fructum ventris tui, nobis post hoc exsilium ostende. O clemens, O pia, O dulcis Virgo Maria.

V. Ora pro nobis, Sancta Dei Genitrix.

R. Ut digni efficiamur promissionibus Christi.

Guardian Angel Prayer

Angel of God, my guardian dear, to whom God's love commits me here, ever this day be at my side, to light and guard, to rule and guide. Amen.

The Confiteor

I confess to almighty God and to you, my brothers and sisters, that I have greatly sinned in my thoughts and in my words, in what I have done and in what I have failed to do, through my fault, through my fault, through my most grievous fault; therefore I ask blessed Mary ever-Virgin, all the angels and saints, and you, my brothers and sisters, to pray for me to the Lord our God.

Act of Contrition

O my God, I am heartily sorry for having offended Thee, and I detest all my sins because I dread the loss of heaven and the pains of hell, but most of all because they offend Thee, my God, Who art all good and deserving of all my love. I firmly resolve, with the help of Thy grace, to sin no more and avoid the near occasions of sin. Amen.

Prayer before a Day's Work

Direct, we beg You, O Lord, our actions by Your holy inspirations, and grant that we may carry them out with Your gracious assistance, that every prayer and work of ours may begin always with You and through You be happily ended. Amen.

Grace before Meals

Bless us, O Lord, and these Thy gifts, which we are about to receive, from Thy bounty, through Christ our Lord. Amen.

Grace after Meals

We give Thee thanks for all Thy benefits, Almighty God, Who lives and reigns forever. And may the souls of the faithful departed, through the mercy of God, rest in peace. Amen.

Mary, Mother of Grace

Mary, Mother of grace, Mother of mercy, shield me from the enemy and receive me at the hour of my death. Amen.

Memorare

Remember, O most gracious Virgin Mary, that never was it known that anyone who fled to thy protection, implored thy help, or sought thine intercession, was left unaided. Inspired by this confidence, I fly unto thee, O Virgin of virgins, my mother; to thee do I come, before thee I stand, sinful and sorrowful. O Mother of the Word Incarnate, despise not my petitions, but in thy mercy hear and answer me. Amen.

We Fly to Thy Protection (Sub tuum praesidium)

We fly to thy protection, O holy Mother of God. Despise not our petitions in our necessities, but deliver us always from all dangers, O glorious and blessed Virgin. Amen.

Consecration to the Blessed Virgin

My Queen and my Mother, I give myself entirely to you, and, in proof of my affection, I give you my eyes, my ears, my tongue, my heart, my whole being without reserve. Since I am your own, keep me and guard me as your property and possession. Amen.

Alma Redemptoris Mater

Loving mother of the Redeemer, gate of heaven, star of the sea, assist your people who have fallen yet strive to rise again. To the wonderment of nature you bore your Creator, yet remained a virgin after as before. You who received Gabriel's joyful greeting, have pity on us poor sinners.

Magnificat

My soul proclaims the greatness of the Lord, my spirit rejoices in God my Savior, for He has looked with favor on His lowly servant. From this day all generations will call me blessed: the Almighty has done great things for me, and holy is His Name. He has mercy on those who fear Him in every generation. He has shown the strength of His arm; He has scattered the proud in their conceit. He has cast down the mighty from their thrones and has lifted up the lowly. He has filled the hungry with good things, and the rich He has sent away empty. He has come to the help of His servant Israel, for He has remembered His promise of mercy, the promise He made to our fathers, to Abraham and his children forever.

Ave Maris Stella

Hail, bright star of ocean, God's own Mother blest, ever sinless Virgin, gate of heavenly rest. Taking that sweet Ave which from Gabriel came, peace confirm within us, changing Eva's name. Break the captives' fetters, light on blindness pour, all our ills expelling, every bliss implore. Show thyself a Mother; may the Word Divine, born for us thy Infant, hear our prayers through thine. Virgin all excelling, mildest of the mild, freed from guilt, preserve us, pure and undefiled. Keep our life all spotless, make our way secure, till we find in Jesus, joy forevermore. Through the highest heaven to the Almighty Three, Father, Son, and Spirit, one same glory be. Amen.

Abandonment to God's Providence

My Lord and my God: into Your hands I abandon the past and the present and the future, what is small and what is great, what amounts to a little and what amounts to a lot, things temporal and things eternal. Amen.[77]

Act of Faith

O my God, I firmly believe that Thou art one God in three divine persons, Father, Son, and Holy Spirit; I believe that Thy divine Son became man and died for our sins, and that He shall come to judge the living and the dead. I believe these and all the truths, which the holy Catholic Church teaches, because Thou hast revealed them, Who canst neither deceive nor be deceived. Amen.

Act of Hope

O my God, relying on Thy almighty power and infinite mercy and promises, I hope to obtain pardon for my sins, the help of Thy grace, and life everlasting, through the merits of Jesus Christ, my Lord and Redeemer. Amen.

Act of Charity

O my God, I love Thee above all things, with my whole heart and soul, because Thou art all-good and worthy of all love. I love my neighbor as myself for the love of Thee. I forgive all who have injured me, and ask pardon of all whom I have injured. Amen.

Act of Spiritual Communion

My Jesus, I believe that Thou art present in the Blessed Sacrament. I love Thee above all things and I desire Thee in my soul. Since I cannot now receive Thee sacramentally, come at least spiritually into my heart. As though Thou wert already there, I embrace Thee and unite myself wholly to Thee; permit not that I should ever be separated from Thee. Amen.

The Divine Praises

Blessed be God. Blessed be His Holy Name. Blessed be Jesus Christ, true God and true Man. Blessed be the Name of Jesus. Blessed be His Most Sacred Heart. Blessed be His Most Precious Blood. Blessed be Jesus in the Most Holy Sacrament of the Altar. Blessed be the Holy Spirit, the Paraclete. Blessed be the great Mother of God, Mary most holy. Blessed be her holy and immaculate conception. Blessed be her glorious assumption. Blessed be the Name of Mary, Virgin and Mother. Blessed be St. Joseph, her most chaste spouse. Blessed be God in His angels and in His saints. Amen.

Prayer before a Crucifix

Behold, O good and most sweet Jesus, I fall upon my knees before Thee, and with most fervent desire beg and beseech Thee that Thou wouldst impress upon my heart a lively sense of faith, hope, and charity, true repentance for my sins, and a firm resolve to make amends. And with deep affection and grief, I reflect upon Thy five wounds, having before my eyes that which Thy prophet David spoke about Thee, O good Jesus: "They have pierced my hands and feet, they have counted all my bones." Amen.

Prayer for Purity

Jesus, Lover of chastity, Mary, Mother most pure, and Joseph, chaste guardian of the Virgin, to you I come at this hour, begging you to plead with God for me. I earnestly wish to be pure in thought, word, and deed in imitation of Your own holy purity. Obtain for me, then, a deep sense of modesty, which will be reflected in my external conduct. Protect my eyes, the windows of my soul, from anything that might dim the luster of a heart that must mirror only Christ-like purity. And when the "Bread of Angels becomes the Bread of me" in my heart at Holy

Communion, seal it forever against the suggestions of sinful pleasures. Heart of Jesus, Fount of all purity, have mercy on us. Amen.

Prayer for the Pope

V. Let us pray for N., our pope.

R. May the Lord preserve him, and give him life, and make him blessed upon the earth, and deliver him not up to the will of his enemies. (Ps 41:3) Our Father, Hail Mary.

V. Let us pray: O God, Shepherd and Ruler of all Thy faithful people, look mercifully upon Thy servant N., whom Thou hast chosen as shepherd to preside over Thy Church. Grant him, we beseech Thee, that by his word and example, he may edify those over whom he hath charge, so that together with the flock committed to him, he may attain everlasting life. Through Christ our Lord. Amen.

Prayer for Bishops

V. Let us pray for Bishop N.

R. May he stand firm and shepherd his flock in Thy strength, O Lord, in accordance with the sublimity of Thy Name.

V. Let us pray: O God, Pastor and Ruler of all the faithful, look down, in Thy mercy, upon Thy servant N., whom Thou hast appointed to preside over Thy Church, and grant, we beseech Thee, that both by word and example he may edify all those who are under his charge; so that, with the flock entrusted to him, he may arrive at length unto life everlasting. Through Christ our Lord. Amen.

O Sacred Banquet (St. Thomas Aquinas)

O sacred banquet, in which Christ is received, the memory of His Passion is renewed, the mind is filled with grace, and a pledge of future glory is given to us.

Prayer for Priests

O Jesus, Eternal Priest, keep Thy priests within the shelter of Thy Sacred Heart, where none may touch them.

Keep unstained their anointed hands, which daily touch Thy Sacred Body. Keep unsullied their lips, daily purpled with Thy Precious Blood.

Keep pure and unworldly their hearts, sealed with the sublime mark of the priesthood. Let Thy Holy Love surround them from the world's contagion.

Bless their labors with abundant fruit, and may the souls to whom they minister be their joy and consolation here and their everlasting crown hereafter.

Mary, Queen of the Clergy, pray for us: obtain for us numerous and holy priests. Amen.

Prayer for Vocations

Lord Jesus Christ, shepherd of souls, Who called the apostles to be fishers of men, raise up new apostles in Your holy Church. Teach them that to serve You is to reign, to possess You is to possess all things. Kindle in the hearts of our young people the fire of zeal for souls. Make them eager to spread Your kingdom upon earth. Grant them courage to follow You, Who are the Way, the Truth, and the Life; Who live and reign forever and ever. Amen.

Prayer of St. Gertrude the Great

Eternal Father, I offer Thee the most Precious Blood of Thy Divine Son, Jesus, in union with the Masses said throughout the world today, for all the holy souls in purgatory, for sinners everywhere, for sinners in the universal Church, those in my own home, and within my family. Amen.

Prayer to Keep the Presence of God

Lord, God Almighty, You have brought us safely to the beginning of this day. Defend us today by Your mighty power, so that we may not fall into any sin and that all our words may so proceed and all our thoughts and actions be so directed as to be always just in Your sight. Through Christ our Lord. Amen.

Hear Us, Lord

Hear us, Lord, holy Father, almighty and eternal God, and graciously send Your holy angel from heaven to watch over, to cherish, to protect, to abide with, and to defend all who dwell in this house. Through Christ our Lord. Amen.

Prayer to St. Peregrine (Patron against Cancer)

O God, Who gave to St. Peregrine an angel for his companion, the Mother of God for his teacher, and Jesus as the Physician of his malady, grant we beseech You, through his merits, that we may on earth intensely love our holy angel, the blessed Virgin Mary, and our Savior, and in him bless them forever. Grant that we may receive the favor, which we now petition. We ask this through the same Christ our Lord. Amen. (Say 7 Our Fathers, 7 Hail Marys, and 7 Glory Bes with the invocation "St. Peregrine, pray for us.")

Prayer in Honor of the Holy Family

Lord Jesus Christ, Who, being made subject to Mary and Joseph, didst consecrate domestic life by Thine ineffable virtues, grant that we, with the assistance of both, may be taught by the example of Thy Holy Family and may attain to its everlasting fellowship. Who lives and reigns forever. Amen.

To you, O blessed Joseph

To you, O blessed Joseph, do we come in our tribulation, and having implored the help of your most holy spouse, we confidently invoke your patronage also.

Through that charity which bound you to the immaculate Virgin Mother of God and through the paternal love with which you embraced the Child Jesus, we humbly beg you graciously to regard the inheritance which Jesus Christ has purchased by His Blood, and with your power and strength to aid us in our necessities.

O most watchful guardian of the Holy Family, defend the chosen children of Jesus Christ; O most loving father, ward off from us every contagion of error and corrupting influence; O our most mighty protector, be propitious to us and from heaven assist us in our struggle with the power of darkness; and, as once you rescued the Child Jesus from deadly peril, so now protect God's holy Church from the snares of the enemy and from all adversity; shield, too, each one of us by your constant protection, so that, supported by your example and your aid, we may be able to live piously, to die holily, and to obtain eternal happiness in heaven. Amen.

Prayer to St. Joseph the Worker for Employment

God our Father and our Creator, You bestow on us gifts and talents to develop and use in accord with Your will.

Grant to me, through the intercession of St. Joseph the Worker as model and guide, employment and work, that I may, with dignity, provide for those who depend on me for care and support.

Grant me the opportunities to use my energy and my talents and abilities for the good of all and the glory of Your name.

We Have Come (To open a meeting)

We have come, O Lord, Holy Spirit, we have come before You, hampered indeed by our many and grievous sins, but for a special purpose gathered together in Your Name.

Come to us and be with us and enter our hearts.

Teach us what we are to do and where we ought to tend; show us what we must accomplish, in order that, with Your help, we may be able to please You in all things.

May You alone be the author and the finisher of our judgments, Who alone with God the Father and His Son possess a glorious Name.

Do not allow us to disturb the order of justice, You Who love equity above all things. Let not ignorance draw us into devious paths. Let not partiality sway our minds or respect of riches or persons pervert our judgment.

But unite us to You effectually by the gift of Your grace alone, that we may be one in You and never forsake the truth; inasmuch as we are gathered together in Your name, so may we in all things hold fast to justice tempered by mercy, so that in this life our judgment may in no way be at variance with You and in the life to come we may attain to everlasting rewards for deeds well done. Amen.

Come, Holy Spirit, Creator Blest (Veni, Creator)

Come, Holy Spirit, Creator blest, and in our souls take up Your rest; Come with Your grace and heavenly aid to fill the hearts which You have made.

O Comforter, to You we cry; O heavenly gift of God Most High; O fount of life and fire of love and sweet anointing from above.

You in Your sevenfold gifts are known; You, finger of God's hand we own; You, promise of the Father, You Who do the tongue with power imbue.

Kindle our senses from above, and make our hearts o'erflow with love; With patience firm and virtue high, the weakness of our flesh supply.

Far from us drive the foe we dread, and grant us Your peace instead; so shall we not, with You for guide, turn from the path of life aside.

Oh, may Your grace on us bestow the Father and the Son to know; And You, through endless times confessed, of both the eternal Spirit blest.

Now to the Father and the Son, Who rose from death, be glory given, with You, O holy Comforter, henceforth by all in earth and heaven. Amen.

Prayer of Saint Francis of Assisi

Lord, make me an instrument of Your peace. Where there is hatred, let me sow love; where there is injury, pardon; where there is doubt, faith; where there is despair, hope; where there is darkness, light; and where there is sadness, joy. O Divine Master, grant that I may not so much seek to be consoled, as to console; to be understood, as to understand; to be loved, as to love. For it is in giving that we receive; it is in pardoning that we are pardoned; and it is in dying that we are born to eternal life. Amen

Most Sweet Jesus (Iesu dulcissime) Act of Reparation

Most sweet Jesus, Whose overflowing charity for men is requited by so much forgetfulness, negligence, and contempt, behold us prostrate before You, eager to repair by a special act of homage the cruel indifference and injuries to which Your loving Heart is everywhere subject.

Mindful, alas! that we ourselves have had a share in such great indignities, which we now deplore from the depths of our hearts, we humbly ask Your pardon and declare our readiness to atone by voluntary expiation, not only for our own personal offenses, but also for the sins of those, who, straying far from the path of salvation, refuse in their obstinate infidelity to follow You, their Shepherd and Leader, or, renouncing the promises of their Baptism, have cast off the sweet yoke of Your law.

We are now resolved to expiate each and every deplorable outrage committed against You; we are now determined to make amends for the manifold offenses against Christian modesty in unbecoming dress and behavior, for all the foul seductions laid to ensnare the feet of the innocent, for the frequent violations of Sundays and holy-days, and the shocking blasphemies uttered against You and Your saints. We wish also to make amends for the insults to which Your vicar on earth and Your priests are subjected, for the profanation, by conscious neglect or terrible acts of sacrilege, of the very Sacrament of Your divine love, and lastly for the public crimes of nations who resist the rights and teaching authority of the Church which You have founded.

Would that we were able to wash away such abominations with our blood. We now offer, in reparation for these violations of Your divine honor, the satisfaction You once made to Your Eternal Father on the cross and which You continue to renew daily on our altars; we offer it in union with the acts of atonement of Your Virgin Mother and all the saints and of the pious faithful on earth; and we sincerely promise to make recompense, as far as we can with the help of Your grace, for all neglect of Your great love and for the sins we and others have committed in the past. Henceforth, we will live a life of unswerving faith, of purity of conduct, of perfect observance of the precepts of the Gospel, and especially that of charity. We promise to the best of our power to prevent others from offending You and to bring as many as possible to follow You.

O loving Jesus, through the intercession of the Blessed Virgin Mother, our model in reparation, deign to receive the voluntary offering we make of this act of expiation; and by the crowning gift of perseverance keep us faithful unto death in our duty and the allegiance we owe to You, so that we may all one day come to that happy home, where with the Father and the Holy Spirit You live and reign, God, forever and ever. Amen.

Te Deum

O God, we praise You and acknowledge You to be the Supreme Lord. Everlasting Father, all the earth worships You. All the angels, the heavens, and all angelic powers, all the cherubim and seraphim continuously cry to You: Holy, holy, holy, Lord, God of Hosts! Heaven and earth are full of the majesty of Your glory.

The glorious choir of the apostles, the wonderful company of prophets, the white-robed army of martyrs praise You. Holy Church throughout the world acknowledges You: The Father of infinite majesty; Your adorable, true, and only Son; also the Holy Spirit, the Comforter.

O Christ, You are the King of glory! You are the everlasting Son of the Father. When You took it upon Yourself to deliver man, You did not disdain the Virgin's womb. Having overcome the sting of death, You opened the kingdom of heaven to all believers. You sit at the right hand of God in the glory of the Father.

We believe that You will come to be our Judge. We, therefore, beg You to help Your servants whom You have redeemed with Your Precious Blood. Let them be numbered with Your saints in everlasting glory. Save Your people, O Lord, and bless Your inheritance! Govern them, and raise them up forever.

Every day we thank You. And we praise Your name forever; yes, forever and ever. O Lord, deign to keep us from sin this day. Have mercy on us, O Lord, have mercy on us. Let Your mercy, O Lord, be upon us, for we have hoped in You. O Lord, in You I have put my trust; let me never be put to shame.

Hidden God

Hidden God, devoutly I adore You, truly present underneath these veils: All my heart subdues itself before You, since it all before You faints and fails.

Not to sight, or taste, or touch be credit, hearing only do we trust secure; I believe, for God the Son has said it — Word of Truth that ever shall endure.

On the cross was veiled Your Godhead's splendor, here Your manhood lies hidden too; unto both alike my faith I render, and, as sued the contrite thief, I sue.

Though I look not on Your wounds with Thomas, You, my Lord, and You, my God, I call: Make me more and more believe Your promise, hope in You, and love You over all.

O memorial of my Savior dying, Living Bread, that gives life to man; make my soul, its life from You supplying, taste Your sweetness, as on earth it can.

Deign, O Jesus, Pelican of heaven, me, a sinner, in Your Blood to lave, to a single drop of which is given all the world from all its sin to save.

Contemplating, Lord, Your hidden presence, grant me what I thirst for and implore, in the revelation of Your essence to behold Your glory evermore.

Act of Dedication to Christ the King (Pope Pius XI)

Most Sweet Jesus, redeemer of the human race, we are Yours and Yours we wish to be. To bind ourselves to You even more closely, we kneel before You today and offer ourselves to Your Most Sacred Heart.

R. Praise to You, our Savior and our King.

Have mercy on all who have never known You and on all who reject You and refuse to obey You: gentle Lord, draw them to Yourself.

R. Praise to You, our Savior and our King.

Reign over the faithful who have never left You, reign over those who have squandered their inheritance, the prodigal children who now are starving: bring them back to their Father's house.

R. Praise to You, our Savior and our King.

Reign over those who are misled by error or divided by discord. Hasten the day when we shall be one in faith and truth, one flock with You, the one Shepherd. Give to Your Church freedom and peace, and to all nations justice and order. Make the earth resound from pole to pole with a single cry: Praise to the Divine Heart that gained our salvation; glory and honor be His forever and ever. Amen.

R. Praise to You, our Savior and our King.

Prayer for Healing the Family Tree (Fr. John Hampsch)

Heavenly Father, I come before You as Your child, in great need of Your help; I have physical health needs, emotional needs, spiritual needs, and interpersonal needs. Many of my problems have been caused by my own failures, neglect, and sinfulness, for which I humbly beg Your forgiveness, Lord. But I also ask You to forgive the sins of my ancestors whose failures have left their effects on me in the form of unwanted tendencies, behavior patterns, and defects in body, mind, and spirit. Heal me, Lord, of all these disorders.

With Your help I sincerely forgive everyone, especially living or dead members of my family tree, who have directly offended me or my loved ones in any way, or those whose sins have resulted in our present sufferings and disorders. In the name of Your divine Son, Jesus, and in the power of His Holy Spirit, I ask You, Father, to deliver me and my entire family tree from the influence of the evil one. Free all living and dead members of my family tree, including those in adoptive relationships and those in extended family relationships, from every contaminating form of bondage. By Your loving concern for us, heavenly Father, and by the shed blood of Your precious Son, Jesus, I beg You to extend Your blessing to me and to all my living and deceased relatives. Heal every negative effect transmitted through all past generations, and prevent such negative effects in future generations of my family tree.

I symbolically place the cross of Jesus over the head of each person in my family tree and between each generation; I ask You to let the cleansing blood of Jesus purify the bloodlines in my family lineage. Set Your protective angels to encamp around us, and permit Archangel Raphael, the patron of healing, to administer Your divine healing power to all of us, even in areas of genetic disability. Give special power to our family members' guardian angels to heal, protect, guide, and encourage each of us in all our needs. Let Your healing power be released at this very moment, and let it continue as long as Your sovereignty permits.

In our family tree, Lord, replace all bondage with a holy bonding in family love. And let there be an ever-deeper bonding with You, Lord, by the Holy Spirit, to Your Son, Jesus. Let the family of the Holy Trinity pervade our family with its tender, warm, loving presence, so that our family may recognize and manifest that love in all our relationships. All of our unknown needs we include with this petition that we pray in Jesus' precious Name. Amen.

St. Joseph, patron of family life, pray for us.

Prayers for Mass

Prayer to All the Angels and Saints before Mass

Angels, archangels, thrones, dominations, principalities, powers, heavenly virtues, cherubim and seraphim, all saints of God, holy men and women, and you especially my patrons: deign to intercede for me that I may be worthy to offer this sacrifice to almighty God, to the praise and glory of His name, for my own welfare and also that of all His holy Church. Amen.

Prayer of St. Thomas Aquinas before Mass

Almighty and ever-living God, I approach the sacrament of Thy only-begotten Son, our Lord Jesus Christ. I come sick to the Doctor of life, unclean to the Fountain of mercy, blind to the Radiance of eternal light, and poor and needy to the Lord of heaven and earth. Lord, in Thy great generosity, heal my sickness, wash away my defilement, enlighten my blindness, enrich my poverty, and clothe my nakedness. May I receive the Bread of Angels, the King of kings and the Lord of lords, with humble reverence, with the purity and faith, the repentance and love, and the determined purpose that will help to bring me to salvation. May I receive the sacrament of the Lord's body and blood, in its reality and power. Kind God, may I receive the Body of Thy only-begotten Son, our Lord Jesus Christ, born from the womb of the Virgin Mary, and so be received into His mystical body, and numbered among His members. Loving Father, as on my earthly pilgrimage I now receive Thy beloved Son under the veil of a sacrament, may I one day see Him face to face in glory, Who lives and reigns with Thee in the unity of the Holy Spirit, God, forever. Amen.

Prayer of St. Ambrose before Mass

Lord Jesus Christ, I approach Thy banquet table in fear and trembling, for I am a sinner, and dare not rely on my own worth, but only on Thy goodness and mercy. I am defiled by my many sins in body and soul, and by my unguarded thoughts and words. Gracious God of majesty and awe, I seek Thy protection, I look for Thy healing. Poor troubled sinner that I am, I appeal to Thee, the fountain of all mercy. I cannot bear Thy judgment, but I trust in Thy salvation. Lord, I show my wounds to Thee and uncover my shame before Thee. I know my sins are many and great, and they fill me with fear, but I hope in Thy mercies, for they cannot be numbered. Lord Jesus Christ, Eternal King, God and man, crucified for mankind, look upon me with mercy and hear my prayer, for I trust in Thee. Have mercy on me, full of sorrow and sin, for the depth of Thy compassion never ends. Praise to Thee, Saving Sacrifice, offered on the wood of the cross for me and for all mankind. Praise to the noble and precious Blood, flowing from the wounds of my crucified Lord Jesus Christ and washing away the sins of the whole world. Remember, Lord, Thy creature, whom Thou hast redeemed with Thy blood; I repent my sins, and I long to put right what I have done. Merciful Father, take away all my offenses and sins; purify me in body and soul, and make me worthy to taste the Holy of Holies. May Thy Body and Blood, which I intend to receive, although I am unworthy, be for me the remission of my sins, the washing away of my guilt, the end of my evil thoughts, and the rebirth of my better instincts. May it incite me to do the works pleasing to Thee and profitable to my health in body and soul, and be a firm defense against the wiles of my enemies. Amen.

Prayer before Communion by St. Anselm

O Lord Jesus Christ, Son of the Living God, Who according to the will of the Father and with the cooperation of the Holy Spirit hast by Thy death given life unto the world, I adore and revere this Thy holy Body and this Thy holy Blood which was given over and poured forth for the many unto the remission of sins. O merciful Lord, I beg of Thy mercy that through the power of this sacrament Thou willst make me one of that many. Through faith and love make me feel the power of these sacraments so I may experience their saving power. Absolve and free from all sin and punishment of sin Thy servants, Thy handmaidens, myself, all who have confessed their sins to me, those whom I have promised or am obliged to pray for, and so too those who themselves hope or beg to be helped by my prayers with Thee. Make our Church rejoice in Thy constant protection and consolation. Amen.

Golden Arrow Prayer

The Golden Arrow Prayer is meant as an act of reparation for the profanation of Sunday and of Holy Days of Obligation.

May the most holy, most sacred, most adorable, most incomprehensible and unutterable Name of God be always praised, blessed, loved, adored, and glorified in heaven, on earth, and under the earth, by all the creatures of God and by the Sacred Heart of Our Lord Jesus Christ, in the Most Holy Sacrament of the Altar. Amen.

Soul of Christ (Anima Christi) for after Communion

Soul of Christ, sanctify me.
Body of Christ, save me.
Blood of Christ, inebriate me.
Water from the side of Christ, wash me.
Passion of Christ, strengthen me.
O good Jesus, hear me.
Within thy wounds, hide me.
Permit me not to be separated from Thee.
From the wicked foe, defend me.
At the hour of my death, call me.
And bid me come to Thee.
That with all Thy saints,
I may praise Thee
Forever and ever.
Amen.

Prayer of St. Bonaventure for after Communion

Pierce, O most sweet Lord Jesus, my inmost soul with the most joyous and healthful wound of Thy love, with true, serene, and most holy apostolic charity, that my soul may ever languish and melt with love and longing for Thee, that it may yearn for Thee and faint for Thy courts, and long to be dissolved and to be with Thee. Grant that my soul may hunger after Thee, the bread of angels, the refreshment of holy souls, our daily and supersubstantial bread, having all sweetness and savor and every delight of taste; let my heart ever hunger after and feed upon Thee, upon Whom the angels desire to look, and may my inmost soul be filled with the sweetness of Thy savor; may it ever thirst after Thee, the fountain of life, the fountain of wisdom and knowledge, the fountain of eternal light, the torrent of pleasure, the richness of the house of God. May it ever compass Thee, seek Thee, find Thee, run to Thee, attain Thee, meditate upon Thee, speak of Thee, and do all things to the praise and glory of Thy name, with humility and discretion, with love and delight, with ease and affection, and with perseverance unto the end; may Thou alone be ever my hope, my entire assurance, my riches, my delight, my pleasure, my joy, my rest and tranquility, my peace, my sweetness, my fragrance, my sweet savor, my food, my refreshment, my refuge, my help, my wisdom, my portion, my possession, and my treasure, in Whom may my mind and my heart be fixed and firmly rooted immovably henceforth and forever. Amen.

Prayer of Thanksgiving (by St. Thomas Aquinas) for after Communion

I thank You, O holy Lord, almighty Father, eternal God, Who have deigned, not through any merits of mine, but out of the condescension of Your goodness, to satisfy me a sinner, Your unworthy servant, with the precious Body and Blood of Your Son, our Lord Jesus Christ.

I pray that this Holy Communion be not a condemnation to punishment for me, but a saving plea to forgiveness.

May it be to me the armor of faith and the shield of a good will.

May it be the emptying out of my vices and the extinction of all lustful desires; an increase of charity and patience, of humility and obedience, and all virtues; a strong defense against the snares of all my enemies, visible and invisible; the perfect quieting of all my evil impulses of flesh and spirit, binding me firmly to You, the one true God; and a happy ending of my life.

I pray too that You will deign to bring me, a sinner, to that ineffable banquet where You with Your Son and the Holy Spirit, are to Your saints true light, fulfillment of desires, eternal joy, unalloyed gladness, and perfect bliss. Through the same Christ our Lord. Amen.

The Fragrance Prayer for after Communion

Dear Jesus, help me to spread Your fragrance wherever I go. Flood my soul with Your spirit and life. Penetrate and possess my whole being so utterly, that my life may only be a radiance of Yours.

Shine through me, and be so in me that every soul I come in contact with may feel Your presence in my soul. Let them look up and see no longer me, but only Jesus!

Stay with me and then I shall begin to shine as You shine, so to shine as to be a light to others. The light, O Jesus, will be all from You; none of it will be mine. It will be You, shining on others through me.

Let me thus praise You the way You love best, by shining on those around me. Let me preach You without preaching, not by words but by my example, by the catching force of the sympathetic influence of what I do, the evident fullness of the love my heart bears to You. Amen.

Prayer of Surrender (by St. Ignatius of Loyola) for after Communion

Lord Jesus Christ, take all my freedom, my memory, my understanding, and my will. All that I have and cherish Thou hast given me. I surrender it all to be guided by Thy will. Thy grace and Thy love are wealth enough for me. Give me these Lord Jesus and I ask for nothing more. Amen.

Prayer of Padre Pio for after Communion

Stay with me, Lord, for it is necessary to have You present so that I do not forget You. You know how easily I abandon You.

Stay with me, Lord, because I am weak and I need Your strength, that I may not fall so often.

Stay with me, Lord, for You are my life, and without You, I am without fervor.

Stay with me, Lord, for You are my light, and without You, I am in darkness.

Stay with me, Lord, to show me Your will.

Stay with me, Lord, so that I hear Your voice and follow You.

Stay with me, Lord, for I desire to love You very much, and always be in Your company.

Stay with me, Lord, if You wish me to be faithful to You.

Stay with me, Lord, for as poor as my soul is, I wish it to be a place of consolation for You, a nest of Love.

Stay with me, Jesus, for it is getting late and the day is coming to a close, and life passes; death, judgment, eternity approaches. It is necessary to renew my strength, so that I will not stop along the way, and for that, I need You. It is getting late and death approaches. I fear the darkness, the temptations, the dryness, the cross, the sorrows. O how I need You, my Jesus, in this night of exile!

Stay with me tonight, Jesus, in life with all its dangers, I need You.

Let me recognize You as Your disciples did at the breaking of bread, so that the Eucharistic Communion be the light which disperses the darkness, the force which sustains me, the unique joy of my heart.

Stay with me, Lord, because at the hour of my death, I want to remain united to You, if not by Communion, at least by grace and love.

Stay with me, Jesus, I do not ask for divine consolation, because I do not merit it, but, the gift of Your Presence, oh yes, I ask this of You!

Stay with me, Lord, for it is You alone I look for, Your Love, Your Grace, Your Will, Your Heart, Your Spirit, because I love You and ask no other reward but to love You more and more.

With a firm love, I will love You with all my heart while on earth and continue to love You perfectly during all eternity. Amen.

Litany of Humility for after Communion

O Jesus meek and humble of heart, Hear me.
From the desire of being esteemed, Deliver me, Jesus.
From the desire of being loved, Deliver me, Jesus.
From the desire of being extolled, Deliver me, Jesus.
From the desire of being honored, Deliver me, Jesus.
From the desire of being praised, Deliver me, Jesus.
From the desire of being preferred to others, Deliver me, Jesus.
From the desire of being consulted, Deliver me, Jesus.
From the desire of being approved, Deliver me, Jesus.
From the fear of being humiliated, Deliver me, Jesus.
From the fear of being despised, Deliver me, Jesus.
From the fear of suffering rebukes, Deliver me, Jesus.
From the fear of being calumniated, Deliver me, Jesus.
From the fear of being forgotten, Deliver me, Jesus.
From the fear of being ridiculed, Deliver me, Jesus.
From the fear of being wronged, Deliver me, Jesus.
From the fear of being suspected, Deliver me, Jesus.
That others may be loved more than I, Jesus, grant me the grace to desire it.
That others may be esteemed more than I, Jesus, grant me the grace to desire it.
That in the opinion of the world, others may increase, and I may decrease, Jesus, grant me the grace to desire it.
That others may be chosen and I set aside, Jesus, grant me the grace to desire it.

That others may be praised and I unnoticed, Jesus, grant me the grace to desire it.

That others may be preferred to me in everything, Jesus, grant me the grace to desire it.

That others may become holier than I, provided that I become as holy as I should, Jesus, grant me the grace to desire it.

Come, Holy Spirit (Veni, Sancte Spiritus) for after Communion

Come, Holy Spirit, fill the hearts of Thy faithful and enkindle in them the fire of Thy love.

V. Send forth Thy Spirit and they shall be created.

R. And Thou shalt renew the face of the earth.

Let us pray. O God, Who didst instruct the hearts of the faithful by the light of the Holy Spirit, grant us in the same Spirit to be truly wise, and ever to rejoice in His consolation. Through Christ our Lord. Amen.

Prayer to St. Michael the Archangel for after Mass

St. Michael the Archangel, defend us in battle; be our defense against the wickedness and snares of the devil. May God rebuke him, we humbly pray. And do thou, O prince of the heavenly host, by the power of God, thrust into hell Satan and all the evil spirits who prowl about the world seeking the ruin of souls. Amen.

Prayer to the Blessed Virgin Mary for after Mass

O Mary, Virgin and Mother most holy, behold, I have received your most dear Son, Whom you conceived in your immaculate womb, brought forth, nursed, and embraced most tenderly. Behold Him at Whose sight you used to rejoice and be filled with all delight; Him Whom, humbly and lovingly, once again I present and offer to you to be clasped in your arms, to be loved by your heart, and to be offered up to the Most Holy Trinity as the supreme worship of adoration, for your own honor and glory and for my needs and for those of the whole world. I ask you therefore, most loving Mother: entreat for me the forgiveness of all my sins, and, in abundant measure, the grace of serving Him in the future more faithfully, and at the last, final grace, so that with you I may praise Him for all the ages of ages. Amen.

Hail Mary...

Prayer to St. Joseph for after Mass

Guardian of virgins and father, St. Joseph, to whose faithful custody Innocence itself, Christ Jesus, and Mary, Virgin of virgins, was committed, I pray and beseech thee by each of these dear pledges, Jesus and Mary, that, being preserved from all uncleanness, I may with spotless mind, pure heart, and a chaste body, ever serve Jesus and Mary most chastely all the days of my life. Amen.

Prayers before the Blessed Sacrament

O Salutaris (by St. Thomas Aquinas):

O salutaris Hostia, Quae caeli pandis ostium: Bella premunt hostilia, Da robur, fer auxilium.

Uni trinoque Domino Sit sempiterna gloria, Qui vitam sine termino Nobis donet in patria. Amen.

O saving Victim, opening wide, the gate of heaven to man below! Our foes press on from every side; Thine aid supply, Thy strength bestow.

To Thy great name be endless praise, Immortal Godhead, One in Three; Oh, grant us endless length of days, in our true native land with Thee. Amen.

Tantum Ergo (by St. Thomas Aquinas):

Tantum ergo Sacramentum Veneremur cernui: Et antiquum documentum Novo cedat ritui: Praestet fides supplementum Sensuum defectui.

Genitori, Genitoque Laus et jubilatio, Salus, honor, virtus quoque Sit et benedictio: Procedenti ab utroque Compar sit laudatio. Amen.

Down in adoration falling, Lo! the sacred Host we hail, Lo! o'er ancient forms departing, newer rites of grace prevail; Faith for all defects supplying, where the feeble senses fail.

To the everlasting Father, and the Son Who reigns on high, with the Holy Spirit proceeding, forth from each eternally, be salvation, honor, blessing, might, and endless majesty. Amen.

Prayer of St. Alphonsus Liguori to begin Visit:

My Lord Jesus Christ, Who because of Your love for men remain night and day in the Blessed Sacrament, full of pity and of love, awaiting, calling, and welcoming all who come to visit You, I believe that You are present here on the altar. I adore You, and I thank You for all the graces You have bestowed on me, especially for having given me Yourself in this sacrament, for having given me Your most holy Mother Mary to plead for me, and for having called me to visit You in this church.

I now salute Your most loving Heart, and that for three ends: first, in thanksgiving for this great gift; secondly, to make amends to You for all the outrages committed against You in this sacrament by Your enemies; thirdly, I intend by this visit to adore You in all the places on earth in which You are present in the Blessed Sacrament and in which You are least honored and most abandoned.

My Jesus, I love You with my whole heart. I am very sorry for having so many times offended Your infinite goodness. With the help of Your grace, I purpose never to offend You again. And now, unworthy though I am, I consecrate myself to You without reserve. I renounce and give entirely to You my will, my affection, my desires, and all that I possess. For the future, dispose of me and all I have as You please.

All I ask of You is Your holy love, final perseverance, and that I may carry out Your will perfectly. I recommend to You the souls in purgatory, especially those who had the greatest devotion to the Blessed Sacrament and to the Blessed Virgin Mary. I also recommend to You all poor sinners.

Finally, my dear Savior, I unite all my desires with the desires of Your most loving Heart; and I offer them, thus united, to the Eternal Father, and beseech Him, in Your name and for love of You, to accept and grant them.

Prayer of St. Alphonsus Liguori to conclude Visit:

Most holy Virgin Immaculate, my Mother Mary, it is to you, who are the Mother of my Lord, the Queen of the world, the advocate, the hope, and the refuge of sinners, that I have recourse today, I, who most of all am deserving of pity. Most humbly do I offer you my homage, O great Queen, and I thank you for all the graces you have obtained for me until now, and particularly for having saved me from hell, which, by my sins, I have so often deserved.

I love you, O most lovable Lady, and because of my love for you, I promise to serve you always and to do all in my power to win others to love you also. In your hands I place all my hopes; I entrust the salvation of my soul to your care. Accept me as your servant, O Mother of Mercy; receive me under your mantle. And since you have such power with God, deliver me from all temptations, or rather, obtain for me the strength to triumph over them until death. Of you I ask the grace of perfect love for Jesus Christ. Through your help I hope to die a happy death. O my Mother I beg you, by the love you bear my God, to help me at all times, but especially at the last moment of my life. Do not leave me, I beseech you, until you see me safe in heaven, blessing you and singing your mercies for all eternity. Amen, so I hope, so may it be.

Things to do during Private Eucharistic Adoration

The Catholic Center at the University of Georgia recommended the following devotions to help private Eucharistic Adoration become more fruitful.[78]

1. Pray the Psalms or the Liturgy of the Hours: Whether you are praising, giving thanks, asking for forgiveness, or seeking an answer, you'll find an appropriate psalm. The ancient prayer of the Church called the Liturgy of the Hours presents an excellent way to pray through the Book of Psalms throughout the year.

2. Recite the "Jesus Prayer": Say "Lord Jesus, have mercy on me, a sinner," repeatedly as you quiet your heart and mind.

3. Meditate using Scripture: Choose a passage from the Bible. Read the words and ask God to let the passage speak to you. Pay special attention to anything that strikes you and ask God what He wishes for you to draw from that message.

4. Read the life of a saint and pray with him or her: Most holy men and women have had a great devotion to Our Lord in the Eucharist. Therese of Lisieux, Catherine of Siena, Francis of Assisi, Thomas Aquinas, Peter Julian Eymard, Dorothy Day, Mother Teresa of Calcutta, and Baroness Catherine de Hueck are just a few. Read about them and pray their prayers before the Blessed Sacrament.

5. Pour out your heart to Christ and adore Him: Speak to Jesus, aware that you are in His presence, and tell Him all that comes to your mind. Listen for His response. Pray the prayer that St. Francis instructed his brothers to pray whenever they were before the Blessed Sacrament: "I adore You, O Christ, present here and in all the churches of the world, for by Your holy cross You have redeemed the world."

6. Ask for forgiveness and intercede for others: Think of those who have hurt you and request a special blessing for them. Ask God to forgive you for all the times you have neglected or hurt someone else. Bring before the Blessed Sacrament all those who have asked you to pray for them. Ask the Lord to address their concerns.

7. Pray the Rosary: Pope John Paul II reminds us, "... is not the enraptured gaze of Mary as she contemplated the face of the newborn Christ and cradled Him in her arms that unparalleled model of love which should inspire us every time we receive Eucharistic communion?" (*The Church and the Eucharist*, 55). Ask Mary to join you as you gaze on Christ in the Eucharist and as you pray the Rosary.

8. Sit quietly and just "be" in the presence of God: Think of a visit to the Blessed Sacrament as coming to see your best friend. Sit quietly and enjoy being in each other's company. Instead of talking to the Lord, try listening to what He wants to tell you.

APPENDIX THREE:
DEVOTIONS

APPENDIX THREE: DEVOTIONS

Holy Rosary

How to pray the Rosary:
1. Make the Sign of the Cross; pray the Apostles' Creed.
2. Pray the Our Father.
3. Pray 3 Hail Marys.
4. Pray the Glory Be.
5. Announce the first mystery, then pray the Our Father.
6. Pray 10 Hail Marys while meditating on the mystery.
7. Pray the Glory Be followed by the Fatima Prayer.
8. Repeat steps 5, 6, and 7 for the remaining mysteries.
9. Pray the Hail, Holy Queen after the five decades are completed.
10. Pray the optional closing prayers; make the Sign of the Cross.

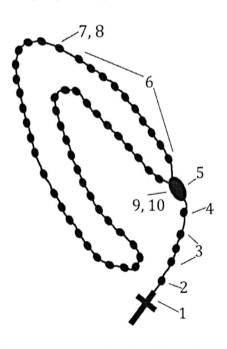

Optional Closing Prayer for the Rosary:

V. Let us pray,

R. O God, Whose only begotten Son, by His life, death, and resurrection, has purchased for us the rewards of eternal salvation, grant, we beseech Thee, that while meditating on these mysteries of the most holy Rosary of the Blessed Virgin Mary, we may imitate what they contain and obtain what they promise, through Christ our Lord. Amen.

Mysteries and Fruits of the Holy Rosary

The Joyful Mysteries

1. The Annunciation — Humility
2. The Visitation — Charity
3. The Nativity of the Lord — Detachment from the World
4. Presentation — Purity
5. Finding of the Child Jesus in the Temple — Obedience to the Will of God

The Luminous Mysteries

1. The Baptism of Jesus — Openness to the Holy Spirit
2. The Miracle at Cana — To Jesus through Mary
3. Proclamation of the Kingdom of God — Repentance, Trust in God
4. Transfiguration — Desire for Holiness
5. Institution of the Eucharist — Eucharistic Adoration

Sorrowful Mysteries

1. Agony in the Garden — Resignation to the Will of God
2. Scourging at the Pillar — Mortification
3. Crowning with Thorns — Moral Courage
4. Carrying of the Cross — Patience in Adversity
5. Crucifixion — Love of Enemies

Glorious Mysteries

1. The Resurrection — Faith
2. The Ascension — Hope
3. The Descent of the Holy Spirit — Love of God
4. The Assumption of Mary — Devotion to Mary
5. The Coronation of the Blessed Virgin Mary — Eternal Happiness

The 15 Promises of Mary to Those Who Recite the Rosary

✠ Whoever shall faithfully serve me by the recitation of the Rosary, shall receive signal graces.

✠ I promise my special protection and the greatest graces to all those who shall recite the Rosary.

✠ The Rosary shall be a powerful armor against hell; it will destroy vice, decrease sin, and defeat heresies.

✠ It will cause virtue and good works to flourish; it will obtain for souls the abundant mercy of God; it will withdraw the heart of men from the love of the world and its vanities and will lift them to the desire of eternal things. Oh, that souls would sanctify themselves by this means!

✠ The soul which recommends itself to me by the recitation of the Rosary shall not perish.

✠ Whoever shall recite the Rosary devoutly, applying himself to the consideration of its sacred mysteries, shall never be conquered by misfortune. God will not chastise him in His justice; he shall not perish by an unprovided death; if he be just he shall remain in the grace of God and become worthy of eternal life.

✠ Whoever shall have a true devotion for the Rosary shall not die without the sacraments of the Church.

✠ Those who are faithful to reciting the Rosary shall have during their life and at their death the light of God and the plenitude of His graces; at the moment of death they shall participate in the merits of the saints in paradise.

✠ I shall deliver from purgatory those who have been devoted to the Rosary.

✠ The faithful children of the Rosary shall merit a high degree of glory in heaven.

✠ You shall obtain all you ask of me by the recitation of the Rosary.

✠ All those who propagate the holy Rosary shall be aided by me in their necessities.

✠ I have obtained from my Divine Son that all the advocates of the Rosary shall have for intercessors the entire celestial court during their life and at the hour of death.

✠ All who recite the Rosary are my sons, and brothers of my only Son Jesus Christ.

✠ Devotion to my Rosary is a great sign of predestination.

54-Day Rosary Novena

Origin of the Novena

The following explanation of the 54-Day Rosary Novena is reprinted from Charles V. Lacey's Rosary Novenas to Our Lady, *which in turn drew material from* The Rosary, My Treasure, *Benedictine Convent, Clyde, Mo.*[79]

This devotion is of comparatively recent origin. In an apparition of Our Lady of Pompeii, which occurred in 1884 at Naples, in the house of Commander Agrelli, the heavenly Mother deigned to make known the manner in which she desires to be invoked.

For 13 months Fortuna Agrelli, the daughter of the commander, had endured dreadful sufferings and torturous cramps; the most celebrated physicians had given her up. On February 16, 1884, the afflicted girl and her relatives commenced a novena of Rosaries. The Queen of the Holy Rosary favored her with an apparition on March 3. Mary, sitting upon a high throne, surrounded by luminous figures, held the divine Child on her lap and in her hand a rosary. The Virgin Mother and the holy Infant were clad in gold embroidered garments. St. Dominic and St. Catherine of Siena accompanied them. The throne was profusely decorated with flowers; the beauty of Our Lady was marvelous.

Mary looked upon the sufferer with maternal tenderness, and the patient saluted her with the words: "Queen of the Holy Rosary, be gracious to me; restore me to health! I have already prayed to thee in a novena, O Mary, but have not yet experienced thy aid. I am so anxious to be cured!"

"Child," responded the Blessed Virgin, "thou hast invoked me by various titles and hast always obtained favors from me. Now, since thou hast called me by that title so pleasing to me, 'Queen of the Holy Rosary,' I can no longer refuse the favor thou dost petition; for this name is most precious and dear to me. Make three novenas, and thou shalt obtain all."

Once more the Queen of the Holy Rosary appeared to her and said, "Whoever desires to obtain favors from me should make three novenas of the prayers of the Rosary, and three novenas in thanksgiving."

The novena consists of five decades of the Rosary each day for 27 days in petition; then immediately after, five decades each day for 27 days in thanksgiving, whether or not the request has been granted.

The meditations vary from day to day. On the first day meditate on the Joyful Mysteries; on the second day the Sorrowful Mysteries; on the third day the Glorious Mysteries; on the fourth day meditate again on the Joyful Mysteries; and so on throughout the 54 days.

The Joyful Mysteries

Prayer before the recitation: Sign of the cross. Hail Mary.

In petition: Hail, Queen of the Most Holy Rosary, my Mother Mary, hail! At thy feet I humbly kneel to offer thee a Crown of Roses, snow white buds to remind thee of thy joys, each bud recalling to thee a holy mystery, each 10 bound together with my petition for a particular grace. O Holy Queen, dispenser of God's graces, and Mother of all who invoke thee, thou canst not look upon my gift and fail to see its binding. As thou receivest my gift, so wilt thou receive my petition; from thy bounty thou wilt give me the favor I so earnestly and trustingly seek. I despair of nothing that I ask of thee. Show thyself my Mother!

In thanksgiving: Hail, Queen of the Most Holy Rosary, my Mother Mary, hail! At thy feet I gratefully kneel to offer thee a Crown of Roses, snow white buds to remind thee of thy joys, each bud recalling to thee a holy mystery, each 10 bound together with my petition for a particular grace. O Holy Queen, dispenser of God's graces, and Mother of all who invoke thee, thou canst not look upon my gift and fail to see its binding. As thou receivest my gift, so wilt thou receive my thanksgiving; from thy bounty thou hast given me the favor I so earnestly and trustingly sought. I despaired not of what I asked of thee, and thou hast truly shown thyself my Mother.

Say: The Apostles' Creed, Our Father, 3 Hail Marys, Glory Be.

The Annunciation: Sweet Mother Mary, meditating on the Mystery of the Annunciation, when the angel Gabriel appeared to thee with the tidings that thou wert to become the Mother of God, greeting thee with that sublime salutation, "Hail, full of grace! The Lord is with thee!" and thou didst humbly submit thyself to the will of the Father, responding, "Behold the handmaid of the Lord. Be it done unto me according to thy word." I humbly pray:

Say: Our Father, 10 Hail Marys, Glory Be.

I bind these snow-white buds with a petition for the virtue of humility and humbly lay this bouquet at thy feet.

The Visitation: Sweet Mother Mary, meditating on the Mystery of the Visitation, when, upon thy visit to thy holy cousin, Elizabeth, she greeted thee with the prophetic utterance, "Blessed art thou among women, and blessed is the fruit of thy womb!" and thou didst answer with that canticle of canticles, the Magnificat. I humbly pray:

Say: Our Father, 10 Hail Marys, Glory Be.

I bind these snow-white buds with a petition for the virtue of charity and humbly lay this bouquet at thy feet.

The Nativity: Sweet Mother Mary, meditating on the Mystery of the Nativity of Our Lord, when, thy time being completed, thou didst bring forth, O holy Virgin, the Redeemer of the world in a stable at Bethlehem; whereupon choirs of angels filled the heavens with their exultant song of praise "Glory to God in the highest, and on earth peace to men of good will." I humbly pray:

Say: Our Father, 10 Hail Marys, Glory Be.

I bind these snow-white buds with a petition for the virtue of detachment from the world and humbly lay this bouquet at thy feet.

The Presentation: Sweet Mother Mary, meditating on the Mystery of the Presentation, when, in obedience to the Law of Moses, thou didst present thy Child in the temple, where the holy prophet Simeon, taking the Child in his arms, offered thanks to God for sparing him to look upon his Savior and foretold thy sufferings by the words: "Thy soul also a sword shall pierce." I humbly pray:

Say: Our Father, 10 Hail Marys, Glory Be.

I bind these snow-white buds with a petition for the virtue of purity and humbly lay this bouquet at thy feet.

The Finding of the Child Jesus in the Temple: Sweet Mother Mary, meditating on the Mystery of the Finding of the Child Jesus in the Temple, when, having sought Him for three days, sorrowing, thy heart was gladdened upon finding Him in the Temple speaking to the doctors; and when, upon thy request, He obediently returned home with thee. I humbly pray:

Say: Our Father, 10 Hail Marys, Glory Be.

I bind these snow-white buds with a petition for the virtue of obedience to the will of God and humbly lay this bouquet at thy feet.

Say: The Hail Holy Queen.

Spiritual Communion: My Jesus, really present in the most holy Sacrament of the Altar, since I cannot now receive Thee under the sacramental veil, I beseech Thee, with a heart full of love and longing, to come spiritually into my soul through the immaculate heart of Thy most holy Mother, and abide with me forever.

Thou in me, and I in Thee, in time and in eternity, in Mary.

In petition: Sweet Mother Mary, I offer thee this spiritual communion to bind my bouquets in a wreath to place upon thy brow. O my Mother! Look with favor upon my gift, and in thy love obtain for me (specify request). Hail Mary ...

In thanksgiving: Sweet Mother Mary, I offer thee this spiritual communion to bind my bouquets in a wreath to place upon thy brow in thanksgiving for (specify request) which thou in thy love hast obtained for me. Hail Mary ...

Prayer: O God! Whose only begotten Son, by His life, death, and resurrection has purchased for us the reward of eternal life, grant, we beseech Thee, that, meditating upon these mysteries of the Most Holy Rosary of the Blessed Virgin Mary, we may imitate what they contain and obtain what they promise. Through the same Christ our Lord. Amen.

May the divine assistance remain always with us. And may the souls of the faithful departed, through the mercy of God, rest in peace. Amen.

Holy Virgin, with thy loving Child, thy blessing give to us this day (night). In the name of the Father, and of the Son, and of the Holy Ghost. Amen.

The Sorrowful Mysteries

Prayer before the recitation: Sign of the cross. Hail Mary.

In petition: Hail, Queen of the Most Holy Rosary, my Mother Mary, hail! At thy feet I humbly kneel to offer thee a Crown of Roses, blood red roses to remind thee of the passion of thy divine Son, with Whom thou didst so fully partake of its bitterness, each rose recalling to thee a holy mystery, each 10 bound together with my petition for a particular grace. O Holy Queen, dispenser of God's graces, and Mother of all who invoke thee! Thou canst not look upon my gift and fail to see its binding. As thou receivest my gift, so wilt thou receive my petition; from thy bounty thou wilt give me the favor I so earnestly and trustingly seek. I despair of nothing that I ask of thee. Show thyself my Mother!

In thanksgiving: Hail, Queen of the Most Holy Rosary, my Mother Mary, hail! At thy feet I gratefully kneel to offer thee a Crown of Roses, blood red roses to remind thee of the passion of thy divine Son, with Whom thou didst so fully partake of its bitterness, each rose recalling to thee a holy mystery, each 10 bound together with my petition for a particular grace. O Holy Queen, dispenser of God's graces, and Mother of all who invoke thee! Thou canst not look upon my gift and fail to see its binding. As thou receivest my gift, so wilt thou receive my thanksgiving; from thy bounty thou hast given me the favor I so earnestly and trustingly sought. I despaired not of what I asked of thee, and thou hast truly shown thyself my Mother.

Say: The Apostles' Creed, Our Father, 3 Hail Marys, Glory Be.

The Agony: O most sorrowful Mother Mary, meditating on the Mystery of the Agony of Our Lord in the Garden, when, in the grotto of the Garden of Olives, Jesus saw the sins of the world unfolded before Him by Satan, who sought to dissuade Him from the sacrifice He was about to make; when, His soul shrinking from the sight, and His precious blood flowing from every pore at the vision of the torture and death He was to undergo, thy own sufferings, dear Mother, the future sufferings of His Church, and His own sufferings in the Blessed Sacrament, He cried in anguish, "Abba! Father! If it be possible, let this chalice pass from Me"; but, immediately resigning Himself to His Father's will, He prayed, "Not as I will, but as Thou wilt!" I humbly pray:

Say: Our Father, 10 Hail Marys, Glory Be.

I bind these blood red roses with a petition for the virtue of resignation to the will of God and humbly lay this bouquet at thy feet.

The Scourging: O most sorrowful Mother Mary, meditating on the Mystery of the Scourging of Our Lord, when, at Pilate's command, thy divine Son, stripped of His garments and bound to a pillar, was lacerated from head to foot with cruel scourges and His flesh torn away until His mortified body could bear no more. I humbly pray:

Say: Our Father, 10 Hail Marys, Glory Be.

I bind these blood red roses with a petition for the virtue of mortification and humbly lay this bouquet at thy feet.

The Crowning With Thorns: O most sorrowful Mother Mary, meditating on the Mystery of the Crowning of Our Lord with Thorns, when, the soldiers, binding about His head a crown of sharp thorns, showered blows upon it, driving the thorns deeply into His head; then, in mock adoration, knelt before Him, crying, "Hail, King of the Jews!" I humbly pray:

Say: Our Father, 10 Hail Marys, Glory Be.

I bind these blood red roses with a petition for the virtue of humility and humbly lay this bouquet at thy feet.

The Carrying of the Cross: O most sorrowful Mother Mary, meditating on the Mystery of the Carrying of the Cross, when, with the heavy wood of the cross upon His shoulders, thy divine Son was dragged, weak and suffering, yet patient, through the streets, amidst the revilements of the people, to Calvary, falling often, but urged along by the cruel blows of His executioners. I humbly pray:

Say: Our Father, 10 Hail Marys, Glory Be.

I bind these blood red roses with a petition for the virtue of patience in adversity and humbly lay this bouquet at thy feet.

The Crucifixion: O most sorrowful Mother Mary, meditating on the Mystery of the Crucifixion, when, having been stripped of His garments, thy divine Son was nailed to the cross, upon which He died after three hours of indescribable agony, during which time He begged from His Father forgiveness for His enemies. I humbly pray:

Say: Our Father, 10 Hail Marys, Glory Be.

I bind these blood red roses with a petition for the virtue of love of our enemies and humbly lay this bouquet at thy feet.

Say: The Hail Holy Queen.

Spiritual Communion: My Jesus, really present in the most holy Sacrament of the Altar, since I cannot now receive Thee under the sacramental veil, I beseech Thee, with a heart full of love and longing, to come spiritually into my soul through the immaculate heart of Thy most holy Mother, and abide with me forever.

Thou in me, and I in Thee, in time and in eternity, in Mary.

In petition: Sweet Mother Mary, I offer thee this spiritual communion to bind my bouquets in a wreath to place upon thy brow. O my Mother! Look with favor upon my gift, and in thy love obtain for me (specify request). Hail Mary ...

In thanksgiving: Sweet Mother Mary, I offer thee this spiritual communion to bind my bouquets in a wreath to place upon thy brow in thanksgiving for (specify request) which thou in thy love hast obtained for me. Hail Mary ...

Prayer: O God! Whose only begotten Son, by His life, death, and resurrection, has purchased for us the reward of eternal life, grant, we beseech Thee, that, meditating upon these mysteries of the Most Holy Rosary of the Blessed Virgin Mary, we may imitate what they contain and obtain what they promise. Through the same Christ our Lord. Amen.

May the divine assistance remain always with us. And may the souls of the faithful departed, through the mercy of God, rest in peace. Amen.

Holy Virgin, with thy loving Child, thy blessing give to us this day (night). In the name of the Father, and of the Son, and of the Holy Ghost. Amen.

The Glorious Mysteries

Prayer before the recitation: Sign of the cross. Hail Mary.

In petition: Hail, Queen of the Most Holy Rosary, my Mother Mary, hail! At thy feet I humbly kneel to offer thee a Crown of Roses, full-blown white roses, tinged with the red of the passion, to remind thee of thy glories, fruits of the sufferings of thy Son and thee, each rose recalling to thee a holy mystery, each 10 bound together with my petition for a particular grace. O Holy Queen, dispenser of God's graces, and Mother of all who invoke thee! Thou canst not look upon my gift and fail to see its binding. As thou receivest my gift, so wilt thou receive my petition; from thy bounty thou wilt give me the favor I so earnestly and trustingly seek. I despair of nothing that I ask of thee. Show thyself my Mother!

In thanksgiving: Hail, Queen of the Most Holy Rosary, my Mother Mary, hail! At thy feet I gratefully kneel to offer thee a Crown of Roses, full-blown white roses, tinged with the red of the passion, to remind thee of thy glories, fruits of the sufferings of thy Son and thee, each rose recalling to thee a holy mystery, each 10 bound together with my petition for a particular grace. O Holy Queen, dispenser of God's graces, and Mother of all who invoke thee! Thou canst not look upon my gift and fail to see its binding. As thou receivest my gift, so wilt thou receive my thanksgiving; from thy bounty thou hast given me the favor I so earnestly and trustingly sought. I despaired not of what I asked of thee, and thou hast truly shown thyself my Mother.

Say: The Apostles' Creed, Our Father, 3 Hail Marys, Glory Be.

The Resurrection: O glorious Mother Mary, meditating on the Mystery of the Resurrection of Our Lord from the Dead, when, on the morning of the third day after His death and burial, He arose from the dead and appeared to thee, dear Mother, and filled thy heart with unspeakable joy, then appeared to the holy women, and to His disciples, who adored Him as their risen God. I humbly pray:

Say: Our Father, 10 Hail Marys, Glory Be.

I bind these full-blown roses with a petition for the virtue of faith and humbly lay this bouquet at thy feet.

The Ascension: O glorious Mother Mary, meditating on the Mystery of the Ascension, when thy divine Son, after 40 days on earth, went to Mount Olivet accompanied by His disciples and thee, where all adored Him for the last time, after which He promised to remain with them until the end of the world, then, extending His pierced hands over all in a last blessing, He ascended before their eyes into heaven. I humbly pray:

Say: Our Father, 10 Hail Marys, Glory Be.

I bind these full-blown roses with a petition for the virtue of hope and humbly lay this bouquet at thy feet.

The Descent of the Holy Spirit: O glorious Mother Mary, meditating on the Mystery of the Descent of the Holy Spirit, when, the apostles being assembled with thee in a house in Jerusalem, the Holy Spirit descended upon them in the form of fiery tongues, inflaming the hearts of the apostles with the fire of divine love, teaching them all truths, giving to them the gift of tongues, and filling thee with the plenitude of His grace, inspired thee to pray for the apostles and the first Christians. I humbly pray:

Say: Our Father, 10 Hail Marys, Glory Be.

I bind these full-blown roses with a petition for the virtue of charity and humbly lay this bouquet at thy feet.

The Assumption of Our Blessed Mother into Heaven: O glorious Mother Mary, meditating on the Mystery of Thy Assumption into Heaven, when, consumed with the desire to be united with thy divine Son in heaven, thy soul departed from thy body and united itself to Him, Who, out of the excessive love He bore for thee, His Mother, whose virginal body was His first tabernacle, took that body into heaven and there, amidst the acclaims of the angels and saints, reinfused into it thy soul. I humbly pray:

Say: Our Father, 10 Hail Marys, Glory Be.

I bind these full-blown roses with a petition for the virtue of union with Christ and humbly lay this bouquet at thy feet.

The Coronation of Our Blessed Mother in Heaven as its Queen: O glorious Mother Mary, meditating on the Mystery of Thy Coronation in Heaven, when, upon being taken up to heaven after thy death, thou wert triply crowned as the august Queen of Heaven by God the Father as His beloved Daughter, by God the Son as His dearest Mother, and by God the Holy Spirit as His chosen Spouse, the most perfect adorer of the Blessed Trinity, pleading our cause as our most powerful and merciful Mother, through thee. I humbly pray:

Say: Our Father, 10 Hail Marys, Glory Be.

I bind these full-blown roses with a petition for the virtue of union with thee and humbly lay this bouquet at thy feet.

Say: The Hail Holy Queen.

Spiritual Communion: My Jesus, really present in the most holy Sacrament of the Altar, since I cannot now receive Thee under the sacramental veil, I beseech Thee, with a heart full of love and longing, to come spiritually into my soul through the immaculate heart of Thy most holy Mother, and abide with me forever.

Thou in me, and I in Thee, in time and in eternity, in Mary.

In petition: Sweet Mother Mary, I offer thee this spiritual communion to bind my bouquets in a wreath to place upon thy brow. O my Mother! Look with favor upon my gift, and in thy love obtain for me (specify request). Hail Mary ...

In thanksgiving: Sweet Mother Mary, I offer thee this spiritual communion to bind my bouquets in a wreath to place upon thy brow in thanksgiving for (specify request) which thou in thy love hast obtained for me. Hail Mary ...

Prayer: O God! Whose only begotten Son, by His life, death, and resurrection, has purchased for us the reward of eternal life, grant, we beseech Thee, that, meditating upon these mysteries of the Most Holy Rosary of the Blessed Virgin Mary, we may imitate what they contain and obtain what they promise. Through the same Christ our Lord. Amen.

May the divine assistance remain always with us. And may the souls of the faithful departed, through the mercy of God, rest in peace. Amen.

Holy Virgin, with thy loving Child, thy blessing give to us this day (night). In the name of the Father, and of the Son, and of the Holy Ghost. Amen.

27-Day Rosary Novena in Petition

J ___ S ___ G ___ J ___ S ___ G ___ J ___ S ___ G ___
J ___ S ___ G ___ J ___ S ___ G ___ J ___ S ___ G ___
J ___ S ___ G ___ J ___ S ___ G ___ J ___ S ___ G ___

27-Day Rosary Novena in Thanksgiving

J ___ S ___ G ___ J ___ S ___ G ___ J ___ S ___ G ___
J ___ S ___ G ___ J ___ S ___ G ___ J ___ S ___ G ___
J ___ S ___ G ___ J ___ S ___ G ___ J ___ S ___ G ___

Pentecost Novena for the Gifts of the Holy Spirit

A novena was first made at the direction of Jesus when He sent His apostles back to Jerusalem to wait for the coming of the Holy Spirit on the first Pentecost. The Pentecost novena is still the only novena (nine days of prayer) officially prescribed by the Church.

The novena begins on the day after the Solemnity of the Ascension, Friday of the Sixth Week of Easter, even if the Solemnity of the Ascension is transferred to the Seventh Sunday of Easter.[80]

Act of Consecration to the Holy Spirit

(To be recited daily during the novena)

On my knees, before the great multitude of heavenly witnesses, I offer myself, soul and body, to You, Eternal Spirit of God. I adore the brightness of Your purity, the unerring keenness of Your justice, and the might of Your love. You are the Strength and Light of my soul. In You I live and move and am. I desire never to grieve You by unfaithfulness to grace, and I pray with all my heart to be kept from the smallest sin against You. Mercifully guard my every thought, and grant that I may always watch for Your light, and listen to Your voice, and follow Your gracious inspirations. I cling to You and give myself to You and ask You, by Your compassion, to watch over me in my weakness. Holding the pierced Feet of Jesus and looking at His five Wounds, and trusting in His Precious Blood and adoring His opened Side and stricken Heart, I implore You, Adorable Spirit, Helper of my infirmity, to keep me in Your grace that I may never sin against You. Give me grace, O Holy Spirit, Spirit of the Father and the Son, to say to You always and everywhere, "Speak Lord for Your servant heareth." Amen.

Prayer for the Seven Gifts of the Holy Spirit

(To be recited daily during the novena)

O Lord Jesus Christ, Who, before ascending into heaven, did promise to send the Holy Spirit to finish Your work in the souls of Your apostles and disciples, deign to grant the same Holy Spirit to me that He may perfect in my soul the work of Your grace and Your love. Grant me the Spirit of Wisdom that I may despise the perishable things of this world and aspire only after the things that are eternal, the Spirit of Understanding to enlighten my mind with the light of Your divine truth, the Spirit on Counsel that I may ever choose the surest way of pleasing God and gaining heaven, the Spirit of Fortitude that I may bear my cross with You and that I may overcome with courage all the obstacles that oppose my salvation, the Spirit of Knowledge that I may know God and know myself and grow perfect in the science of the saints, the Spirit of Piety that I may find the service of God sweet and amiable, and the Spirit of Fear that I may be filled with a loving reverence towards God and may dread in any way to displease Him. Mark me, dear Lord with the sign of Your true disciples, and animate me in all things with Your Spirit. Amen.

First Day: Friday after Ascension or Friday of the Sixth Week of Easter

Holy Spirit! Lord of Light! From Your clear celestial height, Your pure beaming radiance give!

Only one thing is important — eternal salvation. Only one thing, therefore, is to be feared — sin. Sin is the result of ignorance, weakness, and indifference. The Holy Spirit is the Spirit of Light, of Strength, and of Love. With His sevenfold gifts, He enlightens the mind, strengthens the will, and inflames the heart with love of God. To ensure our salvation we ought to invoke the Divine Spirit daily, for "The Spirit helpeth our infirmity. We know not what we should pray for as we ought. But the Spirit Himself asketh for us."

Prayer: Almighty and eternal God, Who hast vouchsafed to regenerate us by water and the Holy Spirit, and hast given us forgiveness of all sins, vouchsafe to send forth from heaven upon us Your sevenfold Spirit, the Spirit of Wisdom and Understanding, the Spirit of Counsel and Fortitude, the Spirit of Knowledge and Piety, and fill us with the Spirit of Holy Fear. Amen.

Our Father... and Hail Mary... (once each), Glory Be... (seven times), Act of Consecration, Prayer for the Seven Gifts.

Second Day: Saturday of the Sixth Week of Easter

Come, Father of the poor; Come, treasures which endure; Come, Light of all that live!

The Gift of Fear: *The Gift of Fear fills us with a sovereign respect for God and makes us dread nothing so much as to offend Him by sin. It is a fear that arises, not from the thought of hell, but from sentiments of reverence and filial submission to our heavenly Father. It is the fear that is the beginning of wisdom, detaching us from worldly pleasures that could in any way separate us from God. "They that fear the Lord will prepare their hearts, and in His sight will sanctify their souls."*

Prayer: Come, O blessed Spirit of Holy Fear, penetrate my inmost heart, that I may set You, my Lord and God, before my face forever. Help me to shun all things that can offend You, and make me worthy to appear before the pure eyes of Your Divine Majesty in heaven, where You live and reign in the unity of the ever Blessed Trinity, God, world without end. Amen.

Our Father... and Hail Mary... (once each), Glory Be... (seven times), Act of Consecration, Prayer for the Seven Gifts.

Third Day: Seventh Sunday of Easter or transferred Ascension

Thou, of all Consolers best, visiting the troubled breast, dost refreshing peace bestow.

The Gift of Piety: *The Gift of Piety begets in our hearts a filial affection for God as our most loving Father. It inspires us to love and respect for His sake persons and things consecrated to Him, as well as those who are vested with His authority, His Blessed Mother and the Saints, the Church and its visible Head, our parents and superiors, our country and its rulers. He who is filled with the Gift of Piety finds the practice of his religion, not a burdensome duty, but a delightful service. "Where there is love, there is no labor."*

Prayer: Come, O Blessed Spirit of Piety, possess my heart. Enkindle therein such a love for God that I may find satisfaction only in His service and for His sake lovingly submit to all legitimate authority. Amen.

Our Father... and Hail Mary... (once each), Glory Be... (seven times), Act of Consecration, Prayer for the Seven Gifts.

Fourth Day: Monday of the Seventh Week of Easter

Thou in toil art comfort sweet, pleasant coolness in the heat, solace in the midst of woe.

The Gift of Fortitude: *By the Gift of Fortitude the soul is strengthened against natural fear and supported to the end in the performance of duty. Fortitude imparts to the will an impulse and energy which move it to undertake without hesitancy the most arduous tasks, to face dangers, to trample under foot human respect, and to endure without complaint the slow martyrdom of even lifelong tribulation. "He that shall persevere unto the end, he shall be saved."*

Prayer: Come, O Blessed Spirit of Fortitude, uphold my soul in time of trouble and adversity, sustain my efforts after holiness, strengthen my weakness, give me courage against all the assaults of my enemies, that I may never be overcome and separated from Thee, my God and greatest Good. Amen.

Our Father... and Hail Mary... (once each), Glory Be... (seven times), Act of Consecration, Prayer for the Seven Gifts.

Fifth Day: Tuesday of the Seventh Week of Easter

Light immortal! Light Divine! Visit Thou these hearts of Thine, and our inmost being fill!

The Gift of Knowledge: *The Gift of Knowledge enables the soul to evaluate created things at their true worth — in their relation to God. Knowledge unmasks the pretense of creatures, reveals their emptiness, and points out their only true purpose as instruments in the service of God. It shows us the loving care of God even in adversity, and directs us to glorify Him in every circumstance of life. Guided by its light, we put first things first and prize the friendship of God beyond all else. "Knowledge is a fountain of life to him that possesseth it."*

Prayer: Come, O Blessed Spirit of Knowledge, and grant that I may perceive the will of the Father; show me the nothingness of earthly things that I may realize their vanity and use them only for Thy glory and my own salvation, looking ever beyond them to Thee and Thy eternal rewards. Amen.

Our Father... and Hail Mary... (once each), Glory Be... (seven times), Act of Consecration, Prayer for the Seven Gifts.

Sixth Day: Wednesday of the Seventh Week of Easter

If Thou take Thy grace away, nothing pure in man will stay, all his good is turn'd to ill.

The Gift of Understanding: *Understanding, as a Gift of the Holy Spirit, helps us to grasp the meaning of the truths* *of our holy religion. By faith we know them, but by Understanding we learn to appreciate and relish them. It enables us to penetrate the inner meaning of revealed truths and through them to be quickened to newness of life. Our faith ceases to be sterile and inactive, but inspires a mode of life that bears eloquent testimony to the faith that is in us; we begin to "walk worthy of God in all things pleasing and increasing in the knowledge of God."*

Prayer: Come, O Spirit of Understanding, and enlighten our minds, that we may know and believe all the mysteries of salvation, and may merit at last to see the eternal light in Thy Light, and in the light of glory to have a clear vision of Thee and the Father and the Son. Amen.

Our Father... and Hail Mary... (once each), Glory Be... (seven times), Act of Consecration, Prayer for the Seven Gifts.

Seventh Day: Thursday of the Seventh Week of Easter

Heal our wounds — our strength renews; On our dryness pour Thy dew, wash the stains of guilt away.

The Gift of Counsel: *The Gift of Counsel endows the soul with supernatural prudence, enabling it to judge promptly and rightly what must done, especially in difficult circumstances. Counsel applies the principles furnished by Knowledge and Understanding to the innumerable concrete cases that confront us in the course of our daily duty as parents, teachers, public servants, and Christian citizens. Counsel is supernatural common sense, a priceless treasure in the quest of salvation. "Above all these things, pray to the Most High, that He may direct thy way in truth."*

Prayer: Come, O Spirit of Counsel, help and guide me in all my ways, that I may always do Thy holy will. Incline my heart to that which is good, turn it away from all that is evil, and direct me by the straight path of Thy commandments to that goal of eternal life for which I long. Amen.

Our Father... and Hail Mary... (once each), Glory Be... (seven times), Act of Consecration, Prayer for the Seven Gifts.

Eighth Day: Friday of the Seventh Week of Easter

Bend the stubborn heart and will, melt the frozen, warm the chill. Guide the steps that go astray!

The Gift of Wisdom: *Embodying all the other gifts, as charity embraces all the other virtues, Wisdom is the most perfect of the gifts. Of wisdom it is written "all good things came to me with her, and innumerable riches through her hands." It is the Gift of Wisdom that strengthens our faith, fortifies hope, perfects charity, and promotes the practice of virtue in the highest degree. Wisdom enlightens the mind to discern and relish things divine, in the appreciation of which earthly joys lose their savor, whilst the Cross of Christ yields a divine sweetness according to the words of the Savior: "Take up thy cross and follow Me, for My yoke is sweet and My burden light."*

Prayer: Come, O Spirit of Wisdom, and reveal to my soul the mysteries of heavenly things, their exceeding greatness, power, and beauty. Teach me to love them above and beyond all the passing joys and satisfactions of earth. Help me to attain them and possess them forever. Amen.

Our Father... and Hail Mary... (once each), Glory Be... (seven times), Act of Consecration, Prayer for the Seven Gifts.

Ninth Day: Saturday of the Vigil of Pentecost

Thou, on those who evermore Thee confess and Thee adore, in Thy sevenfold gift, descend; Give them comfort when they die; give them life with Thee on high; give them joys which never end.

The Fruits of the Holy Spirit: *The Gifts of the Holy Spirit perfect the supernatural virtues by enabling us to practice* *them with greater docility to divine inspiration. As we grow in the knowledge and love of God under the direction of the Holy Spirit, our service becomes more sincere and generous, the practice of virtue more perfect. Such acts of virtue leave the heart filled with joy and consolation and are known as Fruits of the Holy Spirit. These Fruits in turn render the practice of virtue more attractive and become a powerful incentive for still greater efforts in the service of God, to serve Whom is to reign.*

Prayer: Come, O Divine Spirit, fill my heart with Thy heavenly fruits, Thy charity, joy, peace, patience, benignity, goodness, faith, mildness, and temperance, that I may never weary in the service of God, but by continued faithful submission to Thy inspiration, may merit to be united eternally with Thee in the love of the Father and the Son. Amen.

Our Father... and Hail Mary... (once each), Glory Be... (seven times), Act of Consecration, Prayer for the Seven Gifts.

Novena to Mary the Undoer of Knots

Origin of the Novena

Johann Melchior Georg Schmittdner painted Mary Undoer of Knots around 1700. His painting is in the Church of St. Peter in Perlack, Augsburg, Germany. The painting was inspired by St. Irenaeus (Bishop of Lyon martyred in 202) " ... the knot of Eve's disobedience was loosed by the obedience of Mary. For what the virgin Eve had bound fast through unbelief, this did the virgin Mary set free through faith" (*Adversus haereses*, Book III, Chapter 22).

How to Pray the Novena:

1. Make the sign of the cross.
2. Say the Act of Contrition. Ask pardon for your sins and make a firm promise not to commit them again.
3. Say the first three decades of the Rosary.
4. Make the meditation for each day of the novena.
5. Say the last two decades of the Rosary.
6. Finish with the prayer to Our Lady the Undoer of Knots.

Meditations for Each Day of the Novena:

First Day: Dearest Holy Mother, Most Holy Mary, you undo the knots that suffocate your children, extend your merciful hands to me. I entrust to you today this knot (specify request) and all the negative consequences that it provokes in my life. I give you this knot that torments me and makes me unhappy and so impedes me from uniting myself to you and your Son Jesus, my Savior. I run to you, Mary, Undoer of Knots, because I trust you and I know that you never despise a sinning child who comes to ask you for help. I believe that you can undo this knot because Jesus grants you everything. I believe that you want to undo this knot because you are my Mother. I believe that you will do this because you love me with eternal love.

Thank you, dear Mother. Mary, Undoer of Knots, pray for me. *The one who seeks grace, finds it in Mary's hands.*

Second Day: Mary, Beloved Mother, channel of all grace, I return to you today my heart, recognizing that I am a sinner in need of your help. Many times I lose the graces you grant me because of my sins of egoism, pride, rancor, and my lack of generosity and humility. I turn to you today, Mary, Undoer of Knots, for you to ask your Son Jesus to grant me a pure, divested, humble, and trusting heart. I will live today practicing these virtues and offering you this as a sign of my love for you. I entrust into your hands this knot (specify request) which keeps me from reflecting the glory of God. Mary, Undoer of Knots, pray for me. *Mary offered all the moments of her day to God.*

Third Day: Meditating Mother, Queen of Heaven, in whose hands the treasures of the King are found, turn your merciful eyes upon me today. I entrust into your holy hands this knot in my life (specify request) and all the rancor and resentment it has caused in me. I ask Your forgiveness, God the Father, for my sin. Help me now to forgive all the persons who consciously or unconsciously provoked this knot. Give me, also, the grace to forgive myself for having provoked this knot. Only in this way can you undo it. Before you, dearest Mother, and in the name of your Son Jesus, my Savior, Who has suffered so many offenses, having been granted forgiveness, I now forgive these persons...and myself, forever. Thank you, Mary, Undoer of Knots, for undoing the knot of rancor in my heart and the knot which I now present to you. Mary, Undoer of Knots, pray for me. *Turn to Mary, you who desire grace.*

Fourth Day: Dearest Holy Mother, you are generous with all who seek you, have mercy on me. I entrust into your hands this knot which robs the peace of my heart, paralyzes my soul, and keeps me from going to my Lord and serving Him with my life. Undo this knot in my life (specify request) O Mother, and ask Jesus to heal my paralytic faith which gets down-hearted with the stones on the road. Along with you, dearest Mother, may I see these stones as friends, not murmuring against them any longer but giving endless thanks for them. May I smile trustingly in your power. Mary, Undoer of Knots, pray for me. *Mary is the sun, and no one is deprived of her warmth.*

Fifth Day: Mother, Undoer of Knots, generous and compassionate, I come to you today to once again entrust this knot (specify request) in my life to you and to ask the divine wisdom to undo, under the light of the Holy Spirit, this snarl of problems. No one ever saw you angry; to the contrary, your words were so charged with sweetness that the Holy Spirit was manifested on your lips. Take away from me the bitterness, anger, and hatred which this knot has caused me. Give me, O dearest Mother, some of the sweetness and wisdom that is all silently reflected in your heart. And just as you were present at Pentecost, ask Jesus to send me a new presence of the Holy Spirit at this moment in my life. Holy Spirit, come upon me! Mary, Undoer of Knots, pray for me. *Mary, with God, is powerful.*

Sixth Day: Queen of Mercy, I entrust to you this knot in my life (specify request) and I ask you to give me a heart that is patient until you undo it. Teach me to persevere in the living word of Jesus, in the Eucharist, the Sacrament of Confession; stay with me and prepare my heart to celebrate with the angels the grace that will be granted to me. Amen! Alleluia! Mary, Undoer of Knots, pray for me. *You are beautiful, Mary, and there is no stain of sin in you.*

Seventh Day: Mother Most Pure, I come to you today to beg you to undo this knot in my life (specify request) and free me from the snares of evil. God has granted you great power over all the demons. I renounce all of them today, every connection I have had with them, and I proclaim Jesus as my one and only Lord and Savior. Mary, Undoer of Knots, crush the evil one's head and destroy the traps he has set for me by this knot. Thank you, dearest Mother. Most Precious Blood of Jesus, free me! Mary, Undoer of Knots, pray for me. *You are the glory of Jerusalem, the joy of our people.*

Eighth Day: Virgin Mother of God, overflowing with mercy, have mercy on your child and undo this knot (specify request) in my life. I need your visit to my life, like you visited Elizabeth. Bring me Jesus, bring me the Holy Spirit. Teach me to practice the virtues of courage, joyfulness, humility, and faith and, like Elizabeth, to be filled with the Holy Spirit. Make me joyfully rest on your bosom, Mary. I consecrate you as my mother, queen, and friend. I give you my heart and everything I have (my home and family, my material and spiritual goods). I am yours forever. Put your heart in me so that I can do everything Jesus tells me. Mary, Undoer of Knots, pray for me. *Let us go, therefore, full of trust, to the throne of grace.*

Ninth Day: Most Holy Mary, our advocate, undoer of knots, I come today to thank you for undoing this knot in my life (specify request). You know very well the suffering it has caused me. Thank you for coming, Mother, with your long fingers of mercy to dry the tears in my eyes; you receive me in your arms and make it possible for me to receive once again the divine grace. Mary, Undoer of Knots, dearest Mother, I thank you for undoing the knots in my life. Wrap me in your mantle of love; keep me under your protection; enlighten me with your peace! Amen. Mary, Undoer of Knots, pray for me.

Closing Prayer:

Virgin Mary, Mother of fair love, Mother who never refuses to come to the aid of a child in need, Mother whose hands never cease to serve your beloved children because they are moved by the divine love and immense mercy that exists in your heart, cast your compassionate eyes upon me and see the snarl of knots that exist in my life. You know very well how desperate I am, my pain, and how I am bound by these knots. Mary, Mother to whom God entrusted the undoing of the knots in the lives of His children, I entrust into your hands the ribbon of my life. No one, not even the Evil One himself, can take it away from your precious care. In your hands there is no knot that cannot be undone. Powerful Mother, by your grace and intercessory power with your Son and my Liberator, Jesus, take into your hands today this knot (specify request). I beg you to undo it for the glory of God, once for all. You are my hope. O my Lady, you are the only consolation God gives me, the fortification of my feeble strength, the enrichment of my destitution, and with Christ, the freedom from my chains. Hear my plea. Keep me, guide me, protect me, O safe refuge! Mary, Undoer of Knots, pray for me.

Novena to the Sacred Heart

This novena was written by St. Margaret Mary Alacoque and especially favored by St. Padre Pio.

Say once a day for nine days, especially beginning on the Feast of Corpus Christi and ending on the Feast of the Sacred Heart:

O my Jesus, You have said: "Truly I say to you, ask and you will receive; seek and you will find; knock and it will be opened to you." Behold I knock, I seek, and I ask for the grace of (specify request).

Our Father ... Hail Mary ... Glory Be ...

Sacred Heart of Jesus, I place all my trust in You.

O my Jesus, You have said: "Truly I say to you, if you ask anything of the Father in My Name, He will give it to you." Behold, in Your Name, I ask the Father for the grace of (specify request).

Our Father ... Hail Mary ... Glory Be ...

Sacred Heart of Jesus, I place all my trust in You.

O my Jesus, You have said: "Truly I say to you, heaven and earth will pass away but My words will not pass away." Encouraged by Your infallible words I now ask for the grace of (specify request).

Our Father ... Hail Mary ... Glory Be ...

Sacred Heart of Jesus, I place all my trust in You.

Hail, Holy Queen ...

St. Joseph, foster father of Jesus, pray for us.

O Sacred Heart of Jesus, for Whom it is impossible not to have compassion on the afflicted, have pity on us miserable sinners and grant us the grace which we ask of You, through the Sorrowful and Immaculate Heart of Mary, Your tender Mother and ours.

Novena to St. Therese of Lisieux

Novena Prayer

St. Therese, flower of Carmel, you said you would spend your heaven doing good upon the earth. Your trust in God was complete. Listen to my prayer; bring before God my special intention (specify request).

Pray for me that I may have something of your confidence in the loving promises of our God. Pray that I may live my life in union with God's plan for me, and one day see the Face of God Whom you so ardently loved.

St. Therese, you kept your word to love God and to trust the world to that loving providence. Pray for us that we may be faithful to our commitment to love. May our lives, like yours, be able to touch the world and bring it to peace. Amen.

First Day: Loving God, You blessed St. Therese with a great capacity for love. Help us to believe in Your unconditional love for each of us. Amen.

Second Day: Loving God, You were pleased with St. Therese's complete trust in Your care. Help us to rely on Your providential care for us in each circumstance of our lives. Amen.

Third Day: Loving God, You graced St. Therese with the ability to see Your hand in the ordinary routine of each day. Help us to be aware of Your presence in the everyday events of our lives. Amen.

Fourth Day: Loving God, You taught St. Therese how to find a direct way to You through the "little way" of humility and simplicity. Grant that we may never miss the grace that is found in humble service to others. Amen.

Fifth Day: Loving God, You graced St. Therese with the gift of forgiving others even when she felt hurt and betrayed. Help us to be able to forgive others who have wounded us, especially ...

Sixth Day: Loving God, St. Therese experienced each day as a gift from You, as a time for living according to Your will. May we, too, see each new day as a single moment of saying yes to Your will in our lives. Amen.

Seventh Day: Loving God, St. Therese offered to You her frailty and powerlessness. Help us to see in our weakness and our diminishments an opportunity for letting Your light and Your strength be all we need. Amen.

Eighth Day: Loving God, You shepherded St. Therese with Your divine grace and made her a tower of strength to people who had lost faith in You. Help us to be unafraid to pray with confidence for the many in our culture who do not believe. Amen.

Ninth Day: Loving God, St. Therese never doubted that her life had meaning. Help us to understand our possibilities for loving and blessing our children, our elderly parents, our neighbors in need, and for priests throughout the world. Amen.

To conclude this novena, recite one Our Father, one Hail Mary, and one Glory Be.

Act of Oblation to Merciful Love (by St. Therese of Lisieux)

Offering of Myself as a Victim of Holocaust to God's Merciful Love

O My God! Most Blessed Trinity, I desire to love You and make You loved, to work for the glory of Holy Church by saving souls on earth and liberating those suffering in purgatory. I desire to accomplish Your will perfectly and to reach the degree of glory You have prepared for me in Your kingdom. I desire, in a word, to be a saint, but I feel my helplessness and I beg You, O my God, to be Yourself my sanctity!

Since You loved me so much as to give me Your only Son as my Savior and my Spouse, the infinite treasures of His merits are mine. I offer them to You with gladness, begging You to look upon me only in the Face of Jesus and in His heart burning with love.

I offer You, too, all the merits of the saints (in heaven and on earth), their acts of love, and those of the holy angels. Finally, I offer You, O Blessed Trinity, the love and merits of the Blessed Virgin, my dear Mother. It is to her I abandon my offering, begging her to present it to You. Her Divine Son, my Beloved Spouse, told us in the days of His mortal life: "Whatsoever you ask the Father in My name He will give it to you!" I am certain, then, that You will grant my desires; I know, O my God, that the more You want to give, the more You make us desire. I feel in my heart immense desires and it is with confidence I ask You to come and take possession of my soul. Ah! I cannot receive Holy Communion as often as I desire, but, Lord, are You not all-powerful? Remain in me as in a tabernacle and never separate Yourself from Your little victim.

I want to console You for the ingratitude of the wicked, and I beg of You to take away my freedom to displease You. If through weakness I sometimes fall, may Your Divine Glance cleanse my soul immediately, consuming all my imperfections like the fire that transforms everything into itself.

I thank You, O my God, for all the graces You have granted me, especially the grace of making me pass through the crucible of suffering. It is with joy I shall contemplate You on the Last Day carrying the scepter of Your cross. Since You deigned to give me a share in this very precious cross, I hope in heaven to resemble You and to see shining in my glorified body the sacred stigmata of Your passion.

After earth's exile, I hope to go and enjoy You in the fatherland, but I do not want to lay up merits for heaven. I want to work for Your love alone with the one purpose of pleasing You, consoling Your Sacred Heart, and saving souls who will love You eternally.

In the evening of this life, I shall appear before You with empty hands, for I do not ask You, Lord, to count my works. All our justice is stained in Your eyes. I wish, then, to be clothed in Your own justice and to receive from Your love the eternal possession of Yourself. I want no other throne, no other crown but You, my Beloved!

Time is nothing in Your eyes, and a single day is like a thousand years. You can, then, in one instant prepare me to appear before You.

In order to live in one single act of perfect love, I offer myself as a victim of holocaust to Your merciful love, asking You to consume me incessantly, allowing the waves of infinite tenderness shut up within You to overflow into my soul, and that thus I may become a martyr of Your love, O my God!

May this martyrdom, after having prepared me to appear before You, finally cause me to die and may my soul take its flight without any delay into the eternal embrace of Your merciful love.

I want, O my Beloved, at each beat of my heart to renew this offering to You an infinite number of times, until, the shadows having disappeared, I may be able to tell You of my love in an eternal Face to face!

Novena to Divine Mercy

First Day: Today bring to Me all mankind, especially all sinners.

Most Merciful Jesus, Whose very nature it is to have compassion on us and to forgive us, do not look upon our sins but upon our trust which we place in Your infinite goodness. Receive us all into the abode of Your Most Compassionate Heart, and never let us escape from It. We beg this of You by Your love which unites You to the Father and the Holy Spirit.

Eternal Father, turn Your merciful gaze upon all mankind and especially upon poor sinners, all enfolded in the Most Compassionate Heart of Jesus. For the sake of His sorrowful Passion show us Your mercy, that we may praise the omnipotence of Your mercy forever and ever. Amen.

Second Day: Today bring to Me the souls of priests and religious.

Most Merciful Jesus, from Whom comes all that is good, increase Your grace in men and women consecrated to Your service, that they may perform worthy works of mercy and that all who see them may glorify the Father of Mercy Who is in heaven.

Eternal Father, turn Your merciful gaze upon the company of chosen ones in Your vineyard, upon the souls of priests and religious; and endow them with the strength of Your blessing. For the love of the Heart of Your Son in which they are enfolded, impart to them Your power and light, that they may be able to guide others in the way of salvation and with one voice sing praise to Your boundless mercy for ages without end. Amen.

Third Day: Today bring to Me all devout and faithful souls.

Most Merciful Jesus, from the treasury of Your mercy You impart Your graces in great abundance to each and all. Receive us into the abode of Your Most Compassionate Heart and never let us escape from it. We beg this grace of You by that most wondrous love for the Heavenly Father with which Your Heart burns so fiercely.

Eternal Father, turn Your merciful gaze upon faithful souls, as upon the inheritance of Your Son. For the sake of His sorrowful Passion, grant them Your blessing and surround them with Your constant protection. Thus may they never fail in love or lose the treasure of the holy faith, but rather, with all the hosts of angels and saints, may they glorify Your boundless mercy for endless ages. Amen.

Fourth Day: Today bring to Me those who do not believe in God and those who do not yet know Me.

Most compassionate Jesus, You are the Light of the whole world. Receive into the abode of Your Most Compassionate Heart the souls of those who do not believe in God and of those who as yet do not know You. Let the rays of Your grace enlighten them that they, too, together with us, may extol Your wonderful mercy; and do not let them escape from the abode which is Your Most Compassionate Heart.

Eternal Father, turn Your merciful gaze upon the souls of those who do not yet believe in You, and of those who as yet do not know You, but who are enclosed in the Most Compassionate Heart of Jesus. Draw them to the light of the Gospel. These souls do not know what great happiness it is to love You. Grant that they, too, may extol the generosity of Your mercy for endless ages. Amen.

Fifth Day: Today bring to Me the souls of those who have separated themselves from My Church.

Most Merciful Jesus, Goodness Itself, You do not refuse light to those who seek it of You. Receive into the abode of

Your Most Compassionate Heart the souls of those who have separated themselves from Your Church. Draw them by Your light into the unity of the Church, and do not let them escape from the abode of Your Most Compassionate Heart; but bring it about that they, too, come to glorify the generosity of Your mercy.

Eternal Father, turn Your merciful gaze upon the souls of those who have separated themselves from Your Son's Church, who have squandered Your blessings and misused Your graces by obstinately persisting in their errors. Do not look upon their errors, but upon the love of Your own Son and upon His bitter Passion, which He underwent for their sake, since they, too, are enclosed in His Most Compassionate Heart. Bring it about that they also may glorify Your great mercy for endless ages. Amen.

Sixth Day: Today bring to Me the meek and humble souls and the souls of little children.

Most Merciful Jesus, You Yourself have said, "Learn from Me for I am meek and humble of heart." Receive into the abode of Your Most Compassionate Heart all meek and humble souls and the souls of little children. These souls send all heaven into ecstasy and they are the Heavenly Father's favorites. They are a sweet-smelling bouquet before the throne of God; God Himself takes delight in their fragrance. These souls have a permanent abode in Your Most Compassionate Heart, O Jesus, and they unceasingly sing out a hymn of love and mercy.

Eternal Father, turn Your merciful gaze upon meek souls, upon humble souls, and upon little children who are enfolded in the abode which is the Most Compassionate Heart of Jesus. These souls bear the closest resemblance to Your Son. Their fragrance rises from the earth and reaches Your very throne. Father of mercy and of all goodness, I beg You by the love You bear these souls and by the delight You have in them: Bless the whole world, that all souls together may sing out the praises of Your mercy for endless ages. Amen.

Seventh Day: Today bring to Me the souls who especially venerate and glorify My mercy.

Most Merciful Jesus, Whose Heart is Love Itself, receive into the abode of Your Most Compassionate Heart the souls of those who particularly extol and venerate the greatness of Your mercy. These souls are mighty with the very power of God Himself. In the midst of all afflictions and adversities they go forward, confident of Your mercy; and united to You, O Jesus, they carry all mankind on their shoulders. These souls will not be judged severely, but Your mercy will embrace them as they depart from this life.

Eternal Father, turn Your merciful gaze upon the souls who glorify and venerate Your greatest attribute, that of Your fathomless mercy, and who are enclosed in the Most Compassionate Heart of Jesus. These souls are a living Gospel; their hands are full of deeds of mercy, and their hearts, overflowing with joy, sing a canticle of mercy to You, O Most High! I beg You O God: Show them Your mercy according to the hope and trust they have placed in You. Let there be accomplished in them the promise of Jesus, Who said to them that during their life, but especially at the hour of death, the souls who will venerate this fathomless mercy of His, He, Himself, will defend as His glory. Amen.

Eighth Day: Today bring to Me the souls who are detained in purgatory.

Most Merciful Jesus, You Yourself have said that You desire mercy; so I bring into the abode of Your Most Compassionate Heart the souls in purgatory, souls who are very dear to You, and yet, who must make retribution to Your justice. May the streams of Blood and Water which gushed forth from Your Heart put out the flames of purgatory, that there, too, the power of Your mercy may be celebrated.

Eternal Father, turn Your merciful gaze upon the souls suffering in purgatory, who are enfolded in the Most Compassionate Heart of Jesus. I beg You, by the sorrowful Passion of Jesus Your Son, and by all the bitterness with which His most sacred Soul was flooded: Manifest Your mercy to the souls who are under Your just scrutiny. Look upon them in no other way but only through the Wounds of Jesus, Your dearly beloved Son; for we firmly believe that there is no limit to Your goodness and compassion. Amen.

Ninth Day: Today bring to Me souls who have become lukewarm.

Most compassionate Jesus, You are Compassion Itself. I bring lukewarm souls into the abode of Your Most Compassionate Heart. In this fire of Your pure love let these tepid souls, who, like corpses, filled You with such deep loathing, be once again set aflame. O Most Compassionate Jesus, exercise the omnipotence of Your mercy and draw them into the very ardor of Your love, and bestow upon them the gift of holy love, for nothing is beyond Your power.

Eternal Father, turn Your merciful gaze upon lukewarm souls who are nonetheless enfolded in the Most Compassionate Heart of Jesus. Father of Mercy, I beg You by the bitter Passion of Your Son and by His three-hour agony on the cross: Let them, too, glorify the abyss of Your mercy. Amen.

Devotion to the Sacred Heart of Jesus

Origin of the Devotion

Fisheaters.com outlines the history of devotion to the Sacred Heart:[81]

General devotion to the Sacred Heart, the birthplace of the Church and the font of love, were popular in Benedictine and Cistercian monasteries, especially in response to the devotion of St. Gertrude the Great (b. 1256), but specific devotions became even more popularized when St. Margaret Mary Alacoque (1647-1690), a Visitation nun, had a personal revelation involving a series of visions of Christ as she prayed before the Blessed Sacrament. She wrote, "He disclosed to me the marvels of His Love and the inexplicable secrets of His Sacred Heart." Christ emphasized to her His love — and His woundedness caused by man's indifference to this love.

He promised that, in response to those who consecrate themselves and make reparations to His Sacred Heart:

✠ He will give them all the graces necessary in their state of life.

✠ He will establish peace in their homes.

✠ He will comfort them in all their afflictions.

✠ He will be their secure refuge during life, and above all, in death.

✠ He will bestow abundant blessings upon all their undertakings.

✠ Sinners will find in His Heart the source and infinite ocean of mercy.

✠ Lukewarm souls shall become fervent.

✠ Fervent souls shall quickly mount to high perfection.

✠ He will bless every place in which an image of His Heart is exposed and honored.

✠ He will give to priests the gift of touching the most hardened hearts.

✠ Those who shall promote this devotion shall have their names written in His Heart.

✠ In the excessive mercy of His Heart, His all-powerful love will grant to all those who receive Holy Communion on the First Fridays in nine consecutive months the grace of final perseverance; they shall not die in His disgrace, nor without receiving their sacraments. His divine Heart shall be their safe refuge in this last moment.

The devotions attached to these promises are:

✠ Receiving Communion frequently

✠ First Fridays: going to Confession and receiving the Eucharist on the first Friday of each month for nine consecutive months. Many parishes will offer public First Friday devotions; if they do, you must perform First Fridays publicly. If it isn't offered in your parish, you can do this privately, going to Confession, receiving the Eucharist, and offering your prayers for the intentions of the Holy Father.

✠ Holy Hour: Eucharistic Adoration for one hour on Thursdays ("Could you not watch one hour with me?"). Holy Hour can be made alone or as part of a group with formal prayers.

Celebrating the Feast of the Sacred Heart

The Friday that follows the Second Sunday after Pentecost is the Feast of the Sacred Heart, which brings to mind all the attributes of His Divine Heart, mentioned above. Many Catholics prepare for this feast by beginning a Novena to the Sacred Heart on the Feast of Corpus Christi, which is the Thursday of the week before. On the

Feast of the Sacred Heart itself, we can gain a plenary indulgence by making an Act of Reparation to the Sacred Heart (Most Sweet Jesus) (page 177).

Novena to the Sacred Heart

The novena to the Sacred Heart is found on page 231.

Alternative Novena Prayer

O most holy Heart of Jesus, fountain of every blessing, I adore Thee, I love Thee, and with a lively sorrow for my sins, I offer Thee this poor heart of mine. Make me humble, patient, pure, and wholly obedient to Thy will. Grant, good Jesus, that I may live in Thee and for Thee. Protect me in the midst of danger; comfort me in my afflictions; give me health of body, assistance in my temporal needs, Thy blessing on all that I do, and the grace of a holy death. Within Thy Heart I place my every care. In every need let me come to Thee with humble trust saying, "Heart of Jesus help me."

Enthronement of the Sacred Heart

Enthronement of the Sacred Heart is a solemn act of a family giving formal recognition to the kingship of Christ over their family and home and the official, ceremonial beginning of a family's commitment to live out the effects of their recognition of Christ's kingship. During the Enthronement ceremony, a blessed image of the Sacred Heart is hung in the most prominent place in the house and Sacred Scripture is placed before it. Formal prayers are prayed and then each member of the household signs a certificate of the covenant. Contact the National Enthronement Center and ask them for an "Enthronement Kit."

Devotion to the Immaculate Heart of Mary

Origin of the Miraculous Medal

Fisheaters.com outlines the history of devotion to the Immaculate Heart:[82]

Mary appeared to St. Catherine Labouré standing on a globe, rays of light streaming from her fingers, enframed in an oval frame inscribed with the words, "O Mary, conceived without sin, pray for us who have recourse to thee." The whole vision "turned" showing the back of the oval inscribed with the letter "M" entwined with a cross and the hearts of Jesus and Mary, the former surrounded with thorns, the latter pierced with a sword. Twelve stars circled this oval frame. Mary told her to strike a medal in this form — a medal now known as the "Miraculous Medal" — and that all who wore it properly after having it blessed would receive graces. The wearing of the Miraculous Medal has become one of the most common devotions to the Immaculate Heart.

Devotion to the Immaculate Heart of Mary

Devotion to the Immaculate Heart became even more popularized after Mary's appearing to the three young shepherd children at Fatima, Portugal, in 1917 (before the Russian Revolution), when she asked that Russia be consecrated to her Immaculate Heart to prevent the spread of "the errors of Russia." Eight years later, in 1925, Mary appeared to one of the visionaries — Lucia, who had since become a nun — and requested reparations for the various ways in which her Immaculate Heart was offended, such as attacks against her Immaculate Conception, virginity, and divine maternity, and for those who teach their children contempt of Mary or who insult her by desecrating her images.

To make these reparations, she asked that we do five things, all with the intention of making reparation to her Immaculate Heart:

1. Recite at least five decades of the Rosary every day

2. Wear the Brown Scapular (see page 279)

3. Offer our daily duty to God as an act of sacrifice (i.e., make the Morning Offering, page 147)

4. Make five First Saturdays of Reparation to Her Immaculate Heart (see below)

5. The pope, in union with all the bishops of the world, must consecrate Russia to her Immaculate Heart.

The "First Saturdays of Reparation" was not a new devotion, but it became even more popular after Our Lady appeared at Fatima. It consists of, on the first Saturday of each month for five consecutive months:

✠ Going to Confession (within 20 days before or after).

✠ Receiving the Eucharist.

✠ Praying five decades of the Rosary, including the Fatima Prayer.

✠ "Keeping her company" for 15 minutes while meditating on all of the Mysteries of the Rosary with the intention of making reparation to her. This can be done by reading Scripture or other writings relevant to the mysteries, meditating on pictures of the mysteries, or simple meditation.

The promise given by Mary to those who make the First Saturday devotion is her assistance at the hour of death.

Devotion to the Holy Face of Jesus

"By offering My Face to My Eternal Father, nothing will be refused, and the conversion of many sinners will be obtained." — Our Lord to Sr. Marie de Saint-Pierre.

The following information regarding devotion to the Holy Face of Jesus is from Our Lady of the Rosary Library.[83]

Origin of the Devotion to the Holy Face of Jesus

On November 24, 1843, Our Lord spoke the following words to the French Carmelite, Sr. Marie de Saint-Pierre: "The earth is covered with crimes. The violation of the first three commandments of God has irritated My Father. The Holy Name of God blasphemed and the Holy Day of the Lord profaned, fills up the measure in iniquities. These sins have risen unto the Throne of God and provoked His wrath which will soon burst forth if His justice be not appeased. At no time have these crimes reached such a pitch." Our Lord appeared several times to Sister Marie to ask for reparation to be done to His Holy Face.

Sister Marie was given a vision in which she saw the Sacred Heart of Jesus delightfully wounded by the "Golden Arrow" as torrents of graces streamed from It for the conversion of sinners.

The Golden Arrow Prayer

Dictated by Our Lord to Sr. Mary of St. Peter

May the Most Holy, Most Sacred, Most Adorable, Most Incomprehensible and Ineffable Name of God be always praised, blessed, loved, adored, and glorified, in heaven, on earth, and under the earth, by all the creatures of God and by the Sacred Heart of Our Lord Jesus Christ in the Most Holy Sacrament of the altar. Amen.

Our Lord told Sr. Marie of St. Peter on March 16, 1844, "Oh if you only knew what great merit you acquire by saying even once, 'Admirable is the Name of God,' in the spirit of reparation for blasphemy."

Eternal Father, we offer Thee the adorable Face of Thy well-beloved Son, for the honor and glory of Thy Holy Name and for the salvation of souls.

O Jesus, through the merits of Thy Holy Face, have pity on us and on the whole world.

Promises of Our Lord to Sr. Marie of St. Peter

By My Holy Face you shall work wonders.

All those who honor My Holy Face in a spirit of reparation will by so doing perform the office of the pious Veronica.

According to the care you take in making Reparation to My Face, disfigured by blasphemies, so will I take care of yours, which has been disfigured by sin. I will reprint My image and render it as beautiful as it was on leaving the baptismal font.

Our Lord has promised for all those who defend His cause in this work of reparation, by words, by prayers, or in writing, that He will defend them before His Father; at their death He will purify their souls by effacing all the blots of sin and will restore to them their primitive beauty.

Our Lord has promised that He will imprint His Divine likeness on the souls of those who honor His Holy Face.

The Holy Face Medal

Sr. Maria Pierina de Micheli (d. 1945, beatified May 30, 2010) was urged in many visions by the Blessed Mother and Jesus Himself to spread the devotion to the Holy Face. The Blessed Virgin Mary appeared to her holding a scapular which on one piece bore the image from the Holy Shroud with the words "*Illumina Domine Vultum Tuum Super Nos*" (May the light of Thy Face, O Lord, shine upon us) and on the other a Host surrounded by rays and the words "*Mane Nobiscum Domine*" (Stay with us, O Lord). Our Lady promised: "All who shall wear a scapular like this and make, if possible, a visit to the Blessed Sacrament every Tuesday in reparation for the outrages that the Holy Face of my Son Jesus received during His Passion and is still receiving in the Holy Eucharist every day, will be strengthened in the faith and be made ready to defend it, will overcome all difficulties, internal and external, and will have a peaceful death under the loving gaze of my Divine Son."

Sister Pierina felt inspired and obtained permission to have a medal cast which Our Lady approved of and granted the same favors and promises as those of the scapular.

The first medal of the Holy Face was offered to Pope Pius XII who approved the devotion and the medal. On April 17, 1958, he declared the Tuesday before Ash Wednesday (Shrove Tuesday) as the Feast of the Holy Face of Jesus as Our Lord had requested.

Chaplet of the Holy Face of Jesus

The chaplet has for its object the honoring of the five senses of our Lord Jesus Christ and of entreating God for the triumph of His Church. The chaplet comes to us from Sr. St. Pierre and is composed of a cross, 39 beads, six of which are large, and 33 of which are small. The 33 small beads represent the 33 years of the mortal life of our Lord. The first 30 recall to mind the 30 years of His private life, and are divided into five decades of six with the intention of honoring the five senses, touch, hearing, sight, smell, and taste of Jesus, which have their seat principally in His Holy Face, rendering homage to all the sufferings our Lord endured in His Face through each one of these senses. A large bead to honor each of the senses precedes each of these five decades of six beads. The three small beads recall the public life of the Savior and honor the wounds of His adorable Face; the large bead preceding them has the same purpose. A medal of the Holy Face completes the chaplet.

To pray this chaplet, start on the crucifix and recite this invocation: "O God, come to my aid: O Lord, make haste to help me," followed by the Glory Be.

On each large bead pray: "My Jesus, mercy!"

On each small bead recite: "Let God arise, let His enemies be scattered; let those who hate Him flee before His Holy Face."

Complete the chaplet by repeating the Glory Be seven times, honoring the seven words of Jesus upon the Cross, and the seven dolors of the Immaculate Virgin.

On the medal pray: "O God, our Protector, look on us, and cast Your eyes upon the Face of Your Christ."

Chaplet of Divine Mercy

Origin of the Chaplet of Divine Mercy

TheDivineMercy.org explains the origins of the Chaplet of Divine Mercy:[84]

The message of the Divine Mercy that Sister Faustina received from the Lord was not only directed toward her personal growth in faith but also toward the good of the people. With the command of our Lord to paint an image according to the pattern that Sister Faustina had seen came also a request to have this image venerated, first in the Sisters' chapel and then throughout the world.

The same is true with the revelations of the Chaplet. The Lord requested that this Chaplet be said not only by Sister Faustina but also by others: "Encourage souls to say the Chaplet that I have given you."

The same is true of the revelation of the Feast of Mercy. "The Feast of Mercy emerged from My very depths of tenderness. It is My desire that it solemnly be celebrated on the first Sunday after Easter. Mankind will not have peace until it turns to the fount of My mercy."

These requests of the Lord given to Sister Faustina between 1931 and 1938 can be considered the beginning of the Divine Mercy message and devotion in the new forms.

How to Pray the Chaplet of Divine Mercy (using rosary beads)

1. Make the Sign of the Cross.

2. Say the opening prayers (optional): You expired, Jesus, but the source of life gushed forth for souls, and the ocean of mercy opened up for the whole world. O Fount of Life, unfathomable Divine Mercy, envelop the whole world and empty Yourself out upon us.

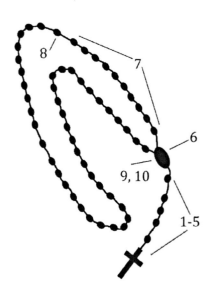

O Blood and Water, which gushed forth from the Heart of Jesus as a fountain of mercy for us, I trust in You! (Repeat three times.)

3. Say an Our Father.

4. Say a Hail Mary.

5. Say the Apostle's Creed.

6. Say an Eternal Father: Eternal Father, I offer You the Body and Blood, Soul and Divinity of Your Dearly Beloved Son, Our Lord, Jesus Christ, in atonement for our sins and those of the whole world.

7. On each of the 10 "Hail Mary" beads of each decade say: For the sake of His sorrowful Passion, have mercy on us and on the whole world.

8. For the remaining decades, repeat the "Eternal Father" (#6) on each "Our Father" bead and the "For the sake of His sorrowful Passion" (#7) on each of the following 10 "Hail Mary" beads.

9. Conclude by repeating three times: Holy God, Holy Mighty One, Holy Immortal One, have mercy on us and on the whole world.

10. Say the closing prayers (optional): Eternal God, in Whom mercy is endless and the treasury of compassion inexhaustible, look kindly upon us and increase Your mercy in us, that in difficult moments we might not despair nor become despondent, but with great confidence submit ourselves to Your holy will, which is Love and Mercy itself.

Chaplet of St. Michael

Origin of the Chaplet of St. Michael[85]

EWTN.com reports that "the history of this chaplet goes back to a devout Servant of God, Antonia d 'Astonac, who had a vision of St. Michael. St. Michael told Antonia to honor him by nine salutations to the nine choirs of angels. St. Michael promised that whoever would practice this devotion in his honor would have, when approaching Holy Communion, an escort of nine angels chosen from each of the nine choirs. In addition, for those who would recite the chaplet daily, he promised his continual assistance and that of all the holy angels during life."

How to pray the chaplet

This chaplet consists of nine sets of three beads, each separated by a larger bead.

O God, come to my assistance. O Lord, make haste to help me. Glory Be ...

Say one Our Father and three Hail Marys after each of the following nine salutations in honor of the nine choirs of angels.

1. By the intercession of St. Michael and the celestial Choir of Seraphim may the Lord make us worthy to burn with the fire of perfect charity. Amen.

2. By the intercession of St. Michael and the celestial Choir of Cherubim may the Lord grant us the grace to leave the ways of sin and run in the paths of Christian perfection. Amen.

3. By the intercession of St. Michael and the celestial Choir of Thrones may the Lord infuse into our hearts a true and sincere spirit of humility. Amen.

4. By the intercession of St. Michael and the celestial Choir of Dominations may the Lord give us grace to

govern our senses and overcome any unruly passions. Amen.

5. By the intercession of St. Michael and the celestial Choir of Virtues may the Lord preserve us from evil and falling into temptation. Amen.

6. By the intercession of St. Michael and the celestial Choir of Powers may the Lord protect our souls against the snares and temptations of the devil. Amen.

7. By the intercession of St. Michael and the celestial Choir of Principalities may God fill our souls with a true spirit of obedience. Amen.

8. By the intercession of St. Michael and the celestial Choir of Archangels may the Lord give us perseverance in faith and in all good works in order that we may attain the glory of heaven. Amen.

9. By the intercession of St. Michael and the celestial Choir of Angels may the Lord grant us to be protected by them in this mortal life and conducted in the life to come to heaven. Amen.

Say one Our Father in honor of each of the following leading angels: St. Michael, St. Gabriel, St. Raphael, and our Guardian Angel.

Concluding prayers:

O glorious prince St. Michael, chief and commander of the heavenly hosts, guardian of souls, vanquisher of rebel spirits, servant in the house of the Divine King, and our admirable conductor, you who shine with excellence and superhuman virtue, deliver us from all evil, who turn to you with confidence, and enable us by your gracious protection to serve God more and more faithfully every day.

Pray for us, O glorious St. Michael, prince of the Church of Jesus Christ, that we may be made worthy of His promises.

Almighty and Everlasting God, Who, by a prodigy of goodness and a merciful desire for the salvation of all men, has appointed the most glorious archangel St. Michael, prince of Your Church, make us worthy, we ask You, to be delivered from all our enemies, that none of them may harass us at the hour of death, but that we may be conducted by him into Your Presence. This we ask through the merits of Jesus Christ Our Lord. Amen.

Stations of the Cross

The following meditations on the Stations of the Cross were written by St. Alphonsus Ligouri.

Preparatory Prayer
(to be said kneeling before the altar)

All: My Lord, Jesus Christ, You have made this journey to die for me with unspeakable love, and I have so many times ungratefully abandoned You. But now I love You with all my heart, and, because I love You, I am sincerely sorry for ever having offended You. Pardon me, my God, and permit me to accompany You on this journey. You go to die for love of me; I want, my beloved Redeemer, to die for love of You. My Jesus, I will live and die always united to You.

At the cross her station keeping, stood the mournful Mother weeping, close to Jesus to the last.

The First Station: Pilate Condemns Jesus to Die

V: We adore You, O Christ, and we praise You. (Genuflect)

R: Because, by Your holy cross, You have redeemed the world. (Rise)

V: Consider how Jesus Christ, after being scourged and crowned with thorns, was unjustly condemned by Pilate to die on the cross. (Kneel)

R: My adorable Jesus, it was not Pilate, no, it was my sins that condemned You to die. I beseech You, by the merits of this sorrowful journey, to assist my soul on its journey to eternity. I love You, beloved Jesus; I love You more than I love myself. With all my heart I repent of ever having offended You. Grant that I may love You always, and then do with me as You will.

(Our Father, Hail Mary, Glory Be.)

Through her heart, His sorrow sharing, all His bitter anguish bearing, now at length the sword has passed.

The Second Station: Jesus Accepts His Cross

V: We adore You, O Christ, and we praise You. (Genuflect)

R: Because, by Your holy cross, You have redeemed the world. (Rise)

V: Consider Jesus as He walked this road with the cross on His shoulders, thinking of us and offering to His Father on our behalf the death He was about to suffer. (Kneel)

R: My most beloved Jesus, I embrace all the sufferings You have destined for me until death. I beg You, by all You suffered in carrying Your cross, to help me carry mine with Your perfect peace and resignation. I love You, Jesus, my love; I repent of ever having offended You. Never let me separate myself from You again. Grant that I may love You always, and then do with me as You will.

(Our Father, Hail Mary, Glory Be.)

O, how sad and sore depressed was that Mother highly blessed of the sole Begotten One.

The Third Station: Jesus Falls the First Time

V: We adore You, O Christ, and we praise You. (Genuflect)

R: Because, by Your holy cross, You have redeemed the world. (Rise)

V: Consider the first fall of Jesus. Loss of blood from the scourging and crowing with thorns had so weakened Him that He could hardly walk, and yet He had to carry that great load upon His shoulders. As the soldiers struck Him cruelly, He fell several times under the heavy cross. (Kneel)

R: My beloved Jesus, it was not the weight of the cross but the weight of my sins which made You suffer so much.

By the merits of this first fall, save me from falling into mortal sin. I love You, O my Jesus, with all my heart; I am sorry that I have offended You. May I never offend You again. Grant that I may love You always, and then do with me as You will.

(Our Father, Hail Mary, Glory Be.)

Christ above in torment hangs. She beneath beholds the pangs of her dying, glorious Son.

The Fourth Station: Jesus Meets His Afflicted Mother

V: We adore You, O Christ, and we praise You. (Genuflect)

R: Because, by Your holy cross, You have redeemed the world. (Rise)

V: Consider how the Son met His Mother on His way to Calvary. Jesus and Mary gazed at each other and their looks became as so many arrows to wound those hearts which loved each other so tenderly. (Kneel)

R: My most loving Jesus, by the pain You suffered in this meeting grant me the grace of being truly devoted to Your most holy Mother. And you, my Queen, who was overwhelmed with sorrow, obtain for me by your prayers a tender and a lasting remembrance of the passion of your divine Son. I love You, Jesus, my Love, above all things. I repent of ever having offended You. Never allow me to offend You again. Grant that I may love You always, and then do with me as You will.

(Our Father, Hail Mary, Glory Be.)

Is there one who would not weep, 'whelmed in miseries so deep, Christ's dear Mother to behold.

The Fifth Station: Simon Helps Jesus Carry the Cross

V: We adore You, O Christ, and we praise You. (Genuflect)

R: Because, by Your holy cross, You have redeemed the world. (Rise)

V: Consider how weak and weary Jesus was. At each step He was at the point of expiring. Fearing that He would die on the way when they wished Him to die the infamous death of the cross, they forced Simon of Cyrene to help carry the cross after Our Lord. (Kneel)

R: My beloved Jesus, I will not refuse the cross as Simon did: I accept it and embrace it. I accept in particular the death that is destined for me with all the pains that may accompany it. I unite it to Your death and I offer it to You. You have died for love of me; I will die for love of You and to please You. Help me by Your grace. I love You, Jesus, my love; I repent of ever having offended You. Never let me offend You again. Grant that I may love You always, and then do with me as You will.

(Our Father, Hail Mary, Glory Be.)

Can the human heart refrain from partaking in her pain, in that Mother's pain untold.

The Sixth Station: Veronica Offers Her Veil to Jesus

V: We adore You, O Christ, and we praise You. (Genuflect)

R: Because, by Your holy cross, You have redeemed the world. (Rise)

V: Consider the compassion of the holy woman, Veronica. Seeing Jesus in such distress, His face bathed in sweat and blood, she presented Him with her veil. Jesus wiped His face and left upon the cloth the image of His sacred countenance. (Kneel)

R: My beloved Jesus, Your face was beautiful before You began this journey, but now it no longer appears beautiful and is disfigured with wounds and blood. Alas, my soul also was once beautiful when it received Your grace in Baptism, but I have since disfigured it with my sins. You alone, my Redeemer, can restore it to its former beauty. Do this by the merits of Your passion, and then do with me as You will.

(Our Father, Hail Mary, Glory Be.)

Bruised, derided, cursed, defiled she beheld her tender Child all with bloody scourges rent.

The Seventh Station: Jesus Falls the Second Time

V: We adore You, O Christ, and we praise You. (Genuflect)

R: Because, by Your holy cross, You have redeemed the world. (Rise)

V: Consider how the second fall of Jesus under His cross renews the pain in all the wounds of the head and members of our afflicted Lord. (Kneel)

R: My most gentle Jesus, how many times You have forgiven me; and how many times I have fallen again and begun again to offend You! By the merits of this second fall, give me the grace to persevere in Your love until death. Grant, that in all my temptations, I may always have recourse to You. I love You, Jesus my love, with all my heart; I am sorry that I have offended You. Never let me offend You again. Grant that I may love You always, and then do with me as You will.

(Our Father, Hail Mary, Glory Be.)

For the sins of His own nation saw Him hang in desolation 'til His spirit forth He sent.

The Eighth Station: Jesus Speaks to the Women

V: We adore You, O Christ, and we praise You. (Genuflect)

R: Because, by Your holy cross, You have redeemed the world. (Rise)

V: Consider how the women wept with compassion seeing Jesus so distressed and dripping with blood as He walked along. Jesus said to them, "Weep not so much for me, but rather for Your children." (Kneel)

R: My Jesus, laden with sorrows, I weep for the sins which I have committed against You because of the punishment I deserve for them, and still more because of the displeasure they have caused You, Who have loved me with an infinite love. It is Your love, more than the fear of hell, which makes me weep for my sins. My Jesus, I love You more than myself; I am sorry that I have offended You. Never allow me to offend You again. Grant that I may love You always, and then do with me as You will.

(Our Father, Hail Mary, Glory Be.)

O sweet Mother! Fount of love, touch my spirit from above. Make my heart with yours accord.

The Ninth Station: Jesus Falls the Third Time

V: We adore You, O Christ, and we praise You. (Genuflect)

R: Because, by Your holy cross, You have redeemed the world. (Rise)

V: Consider how Jesus Christ fell for the third time. He was extremely weak and the cruelty of His executioners was excessive; they tried to hasten His steps though He hardly had strength to move. (Kneel)

R: My outraged Jesus, by the weakness You suffered in going to Calvary, give me enough strength to overcome all human respect and all my evil passions which have led me to despise Your friendship. I love You, Jesus my love, with all my heart; I am sorry for ever having offended You. Never permit me to offend You again. Grant that I may love You always, and then do with me as You will.

(Our Father, Hail Mary, Glory Be.)

Make me feel as You have felt. Make my soul to glow and melt with the love of Christ, my Lord.

The Tenth Station: Jesus Is Stripped of His Garments

V: We adore You, O Christ, and we praise You. (Genuflect)

R: Because, by Your holy cross, You have redeemed the world. (Rise)

V: Consider how Jesus was violently stripped of His clothes by His executioners. The inner garments adhered to His lacerated flesh and the soldiers tore them off so roughly that the skin came with them. Have pity for your Savior so cruelly treated and tell Him: (Kneel)

R: My innocent Jesus, by the torment You suffered in being stripped of Your garments, help me to strip myself of all attachment for the things of earth that I may place all my love in You, Who are so worthy of my love. I love You, O Jesus, with all my heart; I am sorry for ever having offended You. Never let me offend You again. Grant that I may love You always, and then do with me as You will.

(Our Father, Hail Mary, Glory Be.)

Holy Mother, pierce me through, in my heart each wound renew of my Savior crucified.

The Eleventh Station: Jesus Is Nailed to the Cross

V: We adore You, O Christ, and we praise You. (Genuflect)

R: Because, by Your holy cross, You have redeemed the world. (Rise)

V: Consider Jesus, thrown down upon the cross: He stretched out His arms and offered to His eternal Father the sacrifice of His life for our salvation. They nailed His hands and feet, and then, raising the cross, left Him to die in anguish. (Kneel)

R: My despised Jesus, nail my heart to the cross that it may always remain there to love You and never leave You again. I love You more than myself; I am sorry for ever having offended You. Never permit me to offend You again. Grant that I may love You always, and then do with me as You will.

(Our Father, Hail Mary, Glory Be.)

Let me share with you His pain, Who for all our sins was slain, Who for me in torments died.

The Twelfth Station: Jesus Dies Upon the Cross

V: We adore You, O Christ, and we praise You. (Genuflect)

R: Because, by Your holy cross, You have redeemed the world. (Rise)

V: Consider how your Jesus, after three hours of agony on the cross, is finally overwhelmed with suffering and, abandoning Himself to the weight of His body, bows His head and dies. (Kneel)

R: My dying Jesus, I devoutly kiss the cross on which You would die for love of me. I deserve, because of my sins, to die a terrible death, but Your death is my hope. By the merits of Your death, give me the grace to die embracing Your feet and burning with love of You. I yield my soul into Your hands. I love You with my whole heart. I am sorry that I have offended You. Never let me offend You again. Grant that I may love You always, and then do with me as You will.

(Our Father, Hail Mary, Glory Be.)

Let me mingle tears with thee, mourning Him Who mourned for me, all the days that I may live.

The Thirteenth Station: Jesus Is Taken Down from the Cross

V: We adore You, O Christ, and we praise You. (Genuflect)

R: Because, by Your holy cross, You have redeemed the world. (Rise)

V: Consider how, after Our Lord had died, He was taken down from the cross by two of His disciples, Joseph and Nicodemus, and placed in the arms of His afflicted Mother. She received Him with unutterable tenderness and pressed Him close to her bosom. (Kneel)

R: O Mother of Sorrows, for the love of Your Son, accept me as Your servant and pray to Him for me. And You, my Redeemer, since You have died for me, allow me to love You, for I desire only You and nothing more. I love You, Jesus my love, and I am sorry that I have offended You. Never let me offend You again. Grant that I may love You always, and then do with me as You will.

(Our Father, Hail Mary, Glory Be.)

By the cross with you to stay, there with you to weep and pray, is all I ask of you to give.

The Fourteenth Station: Jesus Is Placed in the Sepulcher

V: We adore You, O Christ, and we praise You. (Genuflect)

R: Because, by Your holy cross, You have redeemed the world. (Rise)

V: Consider how the disciples carried the body of Jesus to its burial while His holy Mother went with them and arranged it in the sepulcher with her own hands. They then closed the tomb and all departed. (Kneel)

R: Oh, my buried Jesus, I kiss the stone that closes You in. But You gloriously did rise again on the third day. I beg You by Your resurrection that I may be raised gloriously on the last day, to be united with You in heaven, to praise You and love You forever. I love You, Jesus, and I repent of ever having offended You. Grant that I may love You always, and then do with me as You will.

(Our Father, Hail Mary, Glory Be.)

Virgin of all virgins blest! Listen to my fond request: Let me share your grief divine.

Prayer to Jesus Christ Crucified

My good and dear Jesus, I kneel before You, asking You most earnestly to engrave upon my heart a deep and lively faith, hope, and charity, with true repentance for my sins, and a firm resolve to make amends. As I reflect upon Your five wounds and dwell upon them with deep compassion and grief, I recall, good Jesus, the words the Prophet David spoke long ago concerning Yourself: "They pierced My hands and My feet; they have numbered all My bones."

Aspirations

Jesus!

Blessed be God!

Blessed be the name of the Lord!

Divine Heart of Jesus, convert sinners, save the dying, set free the holy souls in purgatory.

Heart of Jesus, burning with love for us, set our hearts on fire with love of Thee.

Heart of Jesus, I put my trust in Thee!

Jesus, I trust in You!

Jesus meek and humble of heart, make my heart like unto Thine.

Heart of Jesus burning with love for us, inflame our hearts with love of Thee.

Sweet Heart of Jesus, be my love.

My God and my All!

My Lord and my God!

My Jesus, mercy!

Sweet Heart of Mary, be my salvation.

Most Sacred Heart of Jesus, have mercy on us.

Jesus, my God, I love Thee above all things.

Jesus, Son of David, have mercy on me.

Jesus, Mary, and Joseph!

Jesus, Mary, and Joseph, I love you. Save souls!

O Mary, conceived without sin, pray for us who have recourse to thee.

My God, unite all minds in the truth and all hearts in charity.

We adore Thee, O Christ, and we bless Thee; because by Thy Holy Cross Thou hast redeemed the world.

Mother of mercy, pray for us.

Mary, our hope, have pity on us.

Queen of the most Holy Rosary, pray for us.

Mother of Perpetual Help, pray for us.

O God, be merciful to me a sinner.

O God, Thou art all-powerful; make me holy.

Through the sign of the Cross deliver us from our enemies, our God.

APPENDIX FOUR:
INDULGENCES & SACRAMENTALS

APPENDIX FOUR: INDULGENCES AND SACRAMENTALS

Indulgences

Requirements for a plenary indulgence:

✠ Do the work while in a state of grace

✠ Receive sacramental Confession within 20 days of the work (several plenary indulgences may be earned per reception)

✠ Receive Eucharistic communion (one plenary indulgence may be earned per reception of Eucharist)

✠ Pray for the pope's intentions (an Our Father and Hail Mary, or other appropriate prayer, is sufficient)

✠ Have no attachment to sin (even venial) — i.e., the Christian makes an act of the will to love God and despise sin

Requirements for a partial indulgence:

✠ Do the work while in a state of grace

✠ Have the general intention of earning an indulgence

Below is a partial list of ways to obtain a plenary indulgence.

Obtainable at any time and in any place:

✠ Adoring the Blessed Sacrament for at least 30 minutes

✠ Devoutly reading Sacred Scripture for at least 30 minutes

✠ Devoutly performing the Stations of the Cross

✠ Reciting the Rosary with members of the family or in a church, oratory, religious community, or pious association

Obtainable on special days:

✠ January 1st — Pray "Veni, Creator" (page 176)

✠ Each Friday of Lent and Passiontide after Communion — Pray the "Prayer before a Crucifix" (page 171)

✠ Holy Thursday — Pray "Tantum Ergo" (page 193)

✠ Good Friday — Venerate a crucifix

✠ Paschal Vigil — Renew baptismal promises

✠ Feast of Pentecost — Pray "Veni, Creator" (page 176)

✠ Feast of Corpus Christi — Pray "Tantum Ergo" (page 193)

✠ Feast of the Sacred Heart of Jesus — Pray "Most Sweet Jesus" (Act of Reparation) (page 177)

✠ November 1-8 — Visit a cemetery and pray for the departed

✠ November 2 (All Souls Day) — Visit a church or oratory

✠ Feast of Christ the King — Recite publicly "Most Sweet Jesus, Redeemer" (Act of Dedication to Christ the King) (page 180)

✠ December 31 — Recite publicly "Te Deum" (page 179)

Obtainable on special occasions in one's life

✠ First Communion — For the recipient and those who attend

✠ Attend a Mission — Hear some of the sermons and be present for the closing

✠ Spiritual Exercises — At least three days in a Spiritual Exercises Retreat

✠ First Mass of a Newly-Ordained Priest — For priest and those who attend

✠ Jubilees of Sacerdotal Ordination (25th, 50th, and 60th) — For priest who renews resolve to fulfill faithfully the duties of his vocation. Also, if there is a Mass, for all who attend.

✠ The Moment of Death — To the faithful in danger of death, who cannot be assisted by a priest to bring them the sacraments and impart the Apostolic Blessing with its plenary indulgence, Holy Mother Church nevertheless grants a plenary indulgence to be acquired at the point of death, provided they are properly disposed and have been in the habit of reciting some prayers during their lifetime. The use of a crucifix or a cross to gain this indulgence is praiseworthy.

Conditions for all indulgences:

Steve Kellmeyer, in his *Calendar of Indulgences*, summarizes the conditions for all indulgences:[86]

✠ Only baptized persons in a state of grace who generally intend to do so may earn indulgences.

✠ Indulgences cannot be applied to the living, but only to the one doing the work or to the dead.

✠ Only one plenary indulgence per day can be earned (except for prayer at the hour of one's own death).

✠ Several partial indulgences can be earned during the same day.

✠ If only part of a work with a plenary indulgence attached is completed, a partial indulgence still obtains.

✠ If the penance assigned in Confession has indulgences attached, the one work can satisfy both penance and indulgence.

✠ Confessors may commute the work or the conditions if the penitent cannot perform them due to legitimate obstacles.

✠ In groups, indulgenced prayer must be recited by at least one member while the others at least mentally follow the prayer.

✠ If speech/hearing impairments make reciting impossible, mental expression or reading of the prayer is sufficient.

✠ For an indulgence attached to a particular day requiring a church visit, the day begins at noon the day before and ends at midnight.

Catholic Sacramentals

Fisheaters.com defines a sacramental as "anything (material object, time, space, ritual) set apart and blessed by the Church to 'excite good thoughts and to increase devotion, and through these movements of the heart to remit venial sin' (Baltimore Catechism). It is a sacred sign, the use of which disposes us to receive the grace of the sacraments and which helps make various aspects of our lives holy.

"They are not talismans, magic rituals, or 'good luck charms' which give us power over God and His creation; their power derives from Grace of God, through the Church's prayers and the piety they dispose one to. ... As signs of the individual's prayers and piety, and because of the power of God to sanctify material things, and space, and time for our benefit, they are powerful and drive away (the) Evil Spirit when properly used."[87]

Holy Water

Holy Water is defined in Fr. John Hardon's *Catholic Dictionary* as a "sacramental blessed by a priest, invoking God's blessing on all who use it. Blessed water is a symbol of spiritual cleansing, and its use is advised in moments of physical danger and against temptations from spiritual enemies. It is common practice to dip one's fingers in holy water and reverently make the Sign of the Cross as one enters a Catholic church and it is recommended for use in the home."[88]

Blessed Salt

Fr. John H. Hampsch of the Claretian Teaching Ministry explains the history and use of blessed salt: "Salt in the ancient world was a precious commodity .... Roman soldiers were partially paid with packets of salt ("sal" in Latin); this was the origin of our word "salary" and of phrases like "worth his salt," etc. Being costly, it was an appropriate offering to God as a "covenant of salt" (Leviticus 2:13; II Chronicles 13:5; Numbers 18:19), used in sacrifices by the Israelites (Ezekiel 43:24), and for the accompanying sacrificial meal (Genesis 31:54). ...

"As a Catholic sacramental, salt blessed by the liturgical prayer of a priest may be used by itself, unmixed, as in exorcisms, and formerly in the exorcistic prayer at Baptism, or it may be mixed with water to make holy water, as the Ritual prescribes (reminiscent of Elisha's miracle). In whichever form, it is intended to be an instrument of grace to preserve one from the corruption of evil occurring as sin, sickness, demonic influence, etc. ...

"Thus used non-superstitiously, modest amounts of salt may be sprinkled in one's bedroom, or across thresholds to prevent burglary, in cars for safety, etc. A few grains in drinking water or used in cooking or as food seasoning often bring astonishing spiritual and physical benefits, as I have personally witnessed many times. As with the use of sacraments, much depends on the faith and devotion of the person using salt or any sacramental. This faith must be Jesus-centered, as was the faith of the blind man in John 9; he had faith in Jesus, not in the mud and spittle used by Jesus to heal him."[89]

Blessed Oil

Just as salt can be blessed, oil can be blessed by a priest and used as a sacramental. Note that blessed oil is not the same as the holy oils used in the sacraments. In the Old Testament, oil was used to anoint people and objects, in the grain offering, in burial, and for cleansing and healing.

Blessed Candles

Fisheaters.com explains the symbolism of candles: "Used as far back as the days of Moses (Exodus 25:31-40) to foreshadow the Messiahs to come, candles for Christians are symbols of the Christ Who has come and Who will come again. The more explicit symbolism of the candles is described by Dom Prosper Guéranger, OSB, in his *Liturgical Year*: 'According to Ivo of Chartres, the wax, which is formed from the juice of flowers by the bee, always considered as the emblem of virginity, signifies the virginal flesh of the Divine Infant, Who diminished not, either by His conception or His birth, the spotless purity of His Blessed Mother. The same holy bishop would have us see, in the flame of our candle, a symbol of Jesus Who came to enlighten our darkness. St. Anselm, Archbishop of Canterbury, speaking on the same mystery, bids us consider three things in the blessed candle: the wax, the wick, and the flame. The wax, he says, which is the production of the virginal bee, is the Flesh of our Lord; the wick, which is within, is His Soul; the flame, which burns on top, is His Divinity.'"[90]

Religious Medals

Fr. William Saunders in his article "Physical Reminders of Our Faith," in the *Arlington Catholic Herald*, explains the practice of wearing religious medals: "In all, the wearing of a religious medal is a good, pious practice which keeps us mindful of the protection and love of the image it bears. Moreover, the consciousness of that image should motivate us to fulfill our religious duties and put our faith into action. Just as a blessed wedding ring is a constant physical reminder to the spouse of his or her vows of fidelity and love, so do these medals provide a constant physical reminder of the love and fidelity we share with Almighty God and the communion of saints."[91]

The Crucifix

Since the crucifix reminds us of Christ's sacrifice and His triumph over sin and death, it is an especially important sacramental.

Scapulars

This explanation of scapulars is reprinted with permission from Fisheaters.com.[92]

A scapular is a sacramental that looks like two small pieces of wool cloth connected by string that is worn over the neck, either under or over one's clothing (typically under the clothing), such that one piece of cloth hangs over the chest, and the second piece of cloth hangs over the back.

They derive from the scapulars which make up part of monastics' religious habits — that ankle-length (front and back), shoulder-wide, apron-like part of the habit that basically consists of a long rectangular piece of material with a hole for the head (some of them have hoods and some had ties under the arms).

Monastic scapulars came, over time, to be called *jugum Christi* (the yoke of Christ), and receiving the scapular (becoming "invested") took on solemn meaning. Abbreviated forms of the full monastic scapulars were to be worn even at night.

Some scapulars have privileges and indulgences attached to wearing them, but like any sacramental (holy water, blessed candles, etc.), scapulars are not magic; their efficacy depends on the proper intentions and faith of the wearer. Only by following through on the promises one makes when becoming invested can the benefits associated with them be had.

They are best thought of as signs of a commitment to do certain things and of one's being a part of a religious community. They act as reminders, too, of these things they signify and of the saints who are parts of the religious community in question. They are reminders to behave with holiness.

The Brown Scapular

"The Brown Scapular of our Lady of Mount Carmel," associated with the Carmelite Order, is the most well-known. In A.D. 16 July 1251, Our Lady appeared to St. Simon Stock in Cambridge, England, after he prayed for help for his order.

She appeared to him with the scapular and said, "Take, beloved son, this scapular of thy order as a badge of my confraternity and for thee and all Carmelites a special sign of grace; whoever dies in this garment will not suffer everlasting fire. It is the sign of salvation, a safeguard in dangers, a pledge of peace and of the covenant."

Whether this happened exactly in this way or not (St. Simon's original descriptions of the vision are not extant and the wording may not be exact), the scapular was given to St. Simon Stock, and the devotion spread and was well-known by the 16th century.

What can be safely believed because of papal decree is the promise known as the "Sabbatine Privilege." The Sabbatine Privilege is the promise that Our Lady will intercede and pray for those in purgatory who, in earthly life:

✠ Wore the scapular in good faith

✠ Were chaste according to their state in life

✠ Daily recited the Divine Office or, with the permission of one's confessor, the Little Office of Our Lady (a shorter form of the Divine Office in honor of the Blessed Virgin Mary, used by certain religious orders and laity. It is similar to the Common of the Blessed Virgin Mary from the Roman Breviary) or the Rosary

✠ Departed earthly life in charity

Any priest can enroll you in the Confraternity of our Lady of Mount Carmel. Just obtain a scapular, take it to him to have it blessed, and express your desire for enrollment.

Warning: Some falsely believe that wearing the Brown Scapular offers some sort of guarantee of salvation because of the legendary words attributed to Our Lady. This is against Church teaching, is superstitious, and a grave error.

Sacramentals are not magical ways to manipulate God; they are Church-instituted rituals/objects that remind us of what we are supposed to be doing/thinking of, that depend on the faith, hope, and love of the user, and which help prepare us to receive God's saving grace. One must do more than "wear the scapular"; one must wear it worthily.

The Medal of St. Benedict

Most of the below is taken from The Life of St. Benedict *booklet by St. Gregory the Great (b.540-d.604).*[93]

There is indeed no medal that possesses such wonderful power and none so highly esteemed by the holy Church as the medal of St. Benedict. Whosoever wears this medal with devotion, trusting to the life-giving power of the holy cross and the merits of the holy Father St. Benedict, may expect the powerful protection of this great patriarch in his spiritual and temporal needs.

Origin of the St. Benedict Medal

The origin of the medal probably dates back to the time of St. Benedict himself, of whom we know that, in his frequent combats with the evil spirit, he generally made use of the sign of the cross and wrought many miracles thereby. He also taught his disciples to use the sign of our redemption against the assaults of Satan and in other dangers. St. Maurus and St. Placidus, his first and most renowned disciples, wrought their numerous miracles through the power of the holy cross and in the name and by the merits of their holy founder.

The Medal of St. Benedict became more widely known through the following wonderful occurrence: Bruno, afterwards Pope Leo IX, had in his youth been bitten by a venomous reptile, in consequence of which he was seriously ill for two months. He had lost the use of speech and was soon reduced to a skeleton. All hopes of his recovery had been abandoned, when suddenly he beheld a luminous ladder that reached to heaven, from which descended a venerable old man wearing the habit of a monk. It was St. Benedict, bearing in his hand a radiant cross, with which he touched the swollen face of Bruno and instantly cured him. Then the apparition disappeared.

Bruno, who had been healed in such a miraculous manner, later on entered the Order of St. Benedict. He ascended the papal throne in the year 1048 under the name of Leo IX and was renowned in the Church for his sanctity, his devotion to the holy cross and to St. Benedict. Through this pope the Medal of St. Benedict was enriched with special blessings, and its veneration spread everywhere. The use of the medal was solemnly approved and recommended to the faithful by Pope Benedict XIV in 1742.

The Power and Effects of the St. Benedict Medal

Let us state here that we do not ascribe any unknown or hidden power to the medal, a power which the superstitious ascribe to their charms. We know wherein its power lies, and we protest that the graces and favors are due, not to the gold or the silver, the brass or aluminum of the medal, but to our faith in the merits of Christ crucified, to the efficacious prayers of the holy Father St. Benedict, and to the blessings which the holy Church bestows upon the medal and upon those who wear it. This medal excludes every power or influence, which is not from above.

The Medal of St. Benedict is powerful to ward off all dangers of body and soul coming from the evil spirit. We are exposed to the wicked assaults of the devil day and night. St. Peter says, "Your adversary the devil, as roaring lion, goeth about seeking whom he may devour" (1 Pt 5:8). In the life of St. Benedict we see how the devil tried to do harm to his soul and body, and also to his spiritual children. Fr. Paul of Moll, saintly Flemish Benedictine wonder-worker (1824-1896), frustrated the evil doings of the spirit of darkness chiefly through the use of the Medal of St. Benedict, which has proved a most powerful protection against the snares and delusions of the old enemy. Missionaries in pagan lands use this medal with so great effect that it has been given the remarkable name, "The devil-chasing medal."

The medal is, therefore, a powerful means:

✠ To destroy witchcraft and all other diabolical influences.

✠ To keep away the spells of magicians, of wicked and evil-minded persons.

✠ To impart protection to persons tempted, deluded, or tormented by evil spirits.

✠ To obtain the conversion of sinners, especially when they are in danger of death.

✠ To serve as an armor in temptations against holy purity.

✠ To destroy the effects of poison.

✠ To secure a timely and healthy birth for children.

✠ To afford protection against storms and lightning.

✠ To serve as an efficacious remedy for bodily afflictions and a means of protection against contagious diseases.

✠ Finally, the medal has often been used with admirable effect even for animals infected with plague or other maladies, and for fields when invaded by harmful insects.

Use of the St. Benedict Medal

It may be worn about the neck, attached to the scapular or the rosary, or otherwise carried devoutly about one's person. For the sick it can be placed on wounds, dipped in medicine or in water which is given to them to drink.

The medal is frequently put into the foundation of houses or in walls, hung over doors, or fastened on stables and barns to call down God's protection and blessing. It is also buried in fields, as the saintly Fr. Paul of Moll advised his friends to do.

No particular ·prayers are prescribed, for the very wearing and use of the medal is considered a silent prayer to God to grant us, through the merits of St.

Benedict, the favors we request. However, for obtaining extraordinary favors, it is highly recommended to perform special devotions in honor of the holy Father St. Benedict, for instance, on Tuesday, on which day the Church commemorates the death of the holy patriarch. The Way of the Cross is also highly recommended or a novena to St. Benedict.

The St. Benedict Medal

On the front side of the medal:

St. Benedict holding his rule; next to him, on a pedestal, the cup that once held poison. The other pedestal is topped by the raven, who is about to carry away the poisoned bread. Above these are the words *Crux s. patris Benedicti* (The cross of our holy Father Benedict).

Some medals also include underneath St. Benedict the words *ex SM Casino MDCCCLXXX* (from holy Monte Cassino, 1880) and around the front of the medal the words *Eius in obitu nostro praesentia muniamur* (May we at our death be fortified by his presence).

On the back side of the medal:

The cross has the letters, C.S.S.M.L. and N.D.S.M.D., standing for *Crux Sacra Sit Mihi Lux* and *Non Draco Sit Mihi Dux* (May the holy cross be for me a light *and* Let not the dragon be my guide).

The four large letters around the cross, C.S.P.B., stand for *Crux Sancti Patris Benedicti* (The cross of the holy Father Benedict).

Above the cross is the word *Pax* (Peace), the Benedictine motto.

Encircling the cross are the letters V.R.S.N.S.M.V. — S.M.Q.L.I.V.B. standing for *Vade retro Satana; nunquam suade mihi vana — Sunt mala quae libas; ipse venena bibas* (Begone Satan! Suggest not to me thy vain things. The drink you offer is evil; drink that poison yourself).

CITATIONS

Note: Selection of quotations does not necessarily imply approval or agreement with the entire work from which the citation was taken.

[1] Pope Benedict XVI, Address to Participants in the Plenary Meeting of the Congregation for the Doctrine of the Faith. 27 January 2012.

[2] Pope Benedict XVI, Words at the Luncheon with the Cardinals, 21 May 2012.

[3] Jones, Kenneth C. *Index of Leading Catholic Indicators: The Church since Vatican II.* Oriens Publishing Co., St. Louis, Mo., 2003.

[4] Kuhner, Jeffrey T. "The fetal solution: Victims of American hedonism counted in millions of unborn," *Washington Times*, 20 January 2011.

[5] St Cyril of Jerusalem, *Mystagogical Catechesis*, 3, 4.

[6] St. John Chrysostom, *Baptismal Catechesis*, 3, 11-12.

[7] Pope John Paul II, *Novo Millennio Ineunte*, Apostolic Letter, 6 January 2000. Quoting Second Vatican Ecumenical Council, *Lumen Gentium*, 40.

[8] Pope John Paul II, *Novo Millennio Ineunte*, Apostolic Letter, 6 January 2000.

[9] Hardon, Fr. John. "Retreat on the Credo: Faith in the Holy Catholic Church and the Communion of Saints," December 1980. The Real Presence Eucharistic Education and Adoration Association.

<http://www.therealpresence.org/archives/Church_Dog
ma/Church_Dogma_052.htm> Accessed 8 May 2012.
[10] Department of the Army, *The Warrior Ethos and Soldier
Combat Skills: Field Manual No. 3-21.75 (21-75).*
CreateSpace, 2008.
[11] Kreeft, Dr. Peter. *How to Win the Culture War: A
Christian Battle Plan for a Society in Crisis.* IVP Books,
2002.
[12] Sister Lucia of Fatima, Interview with Fr. Augustin
Fuentes, 26 December 1957. The Fatima Network.
<http://www.fatima.org/essentials/opposed/frfuentes.a
sp> Accessed 8 May 2012.
[13] Lewis, C.S. *Mere Christianity.* Book 2, Section 2.
[14] Lombardi Jr., Vince. *What It Takes To Be #1.* McGraw-
Hill, reprint, 2003.
[15] Ibid.
[16] Second Vatican Ecumenical Council, *Lumen Gentium*,
42.
[17] Lombardi Jr., Vince. Ibid.
[18] Pope John Paul II, *Ecclesia de Eucharistia*, Encyclical
Letter, 17 April 2003.
[19] Dolan, Archbishop Timothy M., *Called To Be Holy*, Our
Sunday Visitor, Huntington, Ind., 2005.
[20] Baltimore Catechism.
[21] Merton, Thomas. *Seeds of Contemplation.* New
Directions, 1987.
[22] Second Vatican Ecumenical Council, *Lumen Gentium*,
40.
[23] Aumann, Fr. Jordan. *Spiritual Theology.*
<http://archive.org/details/SpiritualTheologyByFr.Jorda
nAumannO.p> Accessed 8 May 2012.
[24] St. John Vianney, *Selected Sermons*, Ash Wednesday.
[25] Origen, *Commentary on John.*
[26] Pope John Paul II, Homily during Holy Mass on Boston
Common, 1 October 1979.

27 Collopy, Michael. *Works of Love Are Works of Peace.* Ignatius Press, San Francisco, Calif., 1996.

28 Barron, Fr. Robert. Sermon 555, "But for Wales...?", 22nd Week in Ordinary Time. <http://www.wordonfire.org/WOF-Radio/Sermons/Sermon-Archive-for-2011/Sermon-555-But-For-Wales-22nd-Week-in.aspx> Accessed 8 May 2012.

29 Ratzinger, Cardinal Joseph. Theological Commentary, *The Message of Fatima.* <http://www.vatican.va/roman_curia/congregations/cfaith/documents/rc_con_cfaith_doc_20000626_message-fatima_en.html> Accessed 8 May 2012.

30 Ratzinger, Cardinal Joseph. *Milestones: Memoirs, 1927-1977.*

31 Barron, Fr. Robert. Sermon 502, "The Narrow Gate." 21st Sunday in Ordinary Time. <http://www.wordonfire.org/WOF-Radio/Sermons/Sermon-Archive-for-2010/Sermon-502-The-Narrow-Gate-21st-Sunday-in.aspx> Accessed 8 May 2012.

32 à Kempis, Thomas. *The Imitation of Christ.* Book 3, Chapter 55.

33 United States Army. "Army Strong," Television Advertisement. <http://www.youtube.com/watch?v=Mav5Yk9K7ts> Accessed 9 May 2012.

34 Hardon, Fr. John. "The Meaning of Virtue in St. Thomas Aquinas," The Real Presence Eucharistic Education and Adoration Association. <http://www.therealpresence.org/archives/Saints/Saints_004.htm> Accessed 8 May 2012.

35 St. Faustina, Diary, 1578.

36 Ratzinger, Cardinal Joseph. Address to Catechists and Religion Teachers, Jubilee of Catechists, 12 December 2000.

<http://www.ewtn.com/new_evangelization/Ratzinger.htm> Accessed 8 May 2012.

[37] Barron, Fr. Robert. *Seven Deadly Sins, Seven Lively Virtues.* 2007. DVD.

[38] Aristotle, *Ethics*, VIII, 5.

[39] The Soldier's Creed of the United States Army

[40] Carpenter, Lea. "The Intellectual Life of a Navy SEAL," *Big Think*. 13 June 2011. <http://bigthink.com/ideas/38832> Accessed 8 May 2012.

[41] Euteneuer, Fr. Thomas. *Exorcism and the Church Militant.* Human Life International, 2010.

[42] Pope Benedict XVI, *Holy Men and Women from the Middle Ages and Beyond.* Ignatius Press, 2012.

[43] St. Faustina, Diary, 742.

[44] Barron, Fr. Robert. Sermon 522, "Priest, Prophet, and King." The Baptism of the Lord. <http://www.wordonfire.org/WOF-Radio/Sermons/Sermon-Archive-for-2011/Sermon-522---Priest,-Prophet,-and-King---The-Bapti.aspx> Accessed 8 May 2012.

[45] Ibid.

[46] Hartch, Todd. "Born for Combat," *The Catholic Thing*, 3 February 2011. Quoting and paraphrasing Pope Leo XIII's *Sapientiae Christianae*. <http://www.thecatholicthing.org/columns/2011/born-for-combat.html> Accessed 8 May 2012.

[47] Chautard, Jean-Baptiste. *Soul of the Apostolate.* Part 4, Section F.

[48] St. Josemaria Escriva, *The Way*. Chapter 28, Number 629.

[49] Levens, Cpl. Jess. "Recruits climb high obstacles for confidence before advancing to 2nd phase." Marine Corps Recruit Depot San Diego, 22 April 2005. <http://www.marines.mil/unit/mcrc/12mcd/sandiego/Pages/2005/Recruits%20climb%20high%20obstacles%

20for%20confidence%20before%20advancing%20to%2
02nd%20phase.aspx> Accessed 8 May 2012.

[50] Pope Benedict XVI. *Jesus of Nazareth.*

[51] St. Josemaria Escriva, *Christ Is Passing By*, Chapter 1, Number 7.

[52] Roman Catechism, II, V, 18.

[53] Pope John Paul II, Address to the Participants in the Course on the Internal Forum Organized by the Tribunal of the Apostolic Penitentiary, 27 March 2004.

[54] University of Navarre, *The Navarre Bible.*

[55] McCloskey, Fr. John, "The Seven Daily Habits of Holy Apostolic People," *CatholiCity*. <http://www.catholicity.com/mccloskey/sevenhabits.html> Accessed 9 May 2012.

[56] Ibid.

[57] St. Josemaria Escriva, *The Way*, Chapter 6, Number 191.

[58] St. Josemaria Escriva, *The Way*, Chapter 3, Number 116.

[59] St. Josemaria Escriva, *Furrow*, Chapter 14, Number 474.

[60] McCloskey, Fr. John, Ibid.

[61] Pope Paul VI, *Indulgentiarum doctrina*, Apostolic Constitution, Chapter 2, Number 5.

[62] Pope John Paul II, Ad Limina meeting with American Bishops Region X, Number 5, 22 May 2004.

[63] *Primer on Indulgences*, Catholic Answers, <http://www.catholic.com/tracts/primer-on-indulgences> Accessed 9 May 2012.

[64] Kellmeyer, Steve, *The Beauty of Grace Calendar of Indulgences 2012*, Bridegroom Press, Plano, Texas, 2012. Available through BridegroomPress.com.

[65] Ibid.

[66] Tassone, Susan. *Praying with the Saints for the Holy Souls in Purgatory,* Our Sunday Visitor, Huntington, Ind., 2009. Excerpt from The Way of the Cross for the Holy Souls in Purgatory by Susan Tassone © Our Sunday Visitor Publishing, 1-800-348-2440, www.osv.com. Used by permission. No

other use of this material is authorized.

[67] Pope Benedict XVI, *Spe Salvi*, Encyclical, Part III, Number 48. 30 November 2007.

[68] St. Faustina, Diary, 187.

[69] Partners in Evangelism, "The Power of Intercessory Prayer," The Word Among Us Inc., Ijamsville, MD, 21754 <http://www.christlife.org/resources/articles/IntercessoryPrayer.html> Accessed 17 May 2012.

[70] Pope John Paul II, Homily at the Canonization of St. Josemaria Escriva de Balaguer, 6 October 2002. Paragraphs 4-5.

[71] Second Vatican Ecumenical Council, *Gaudium et Spes*, 14.

[72] Philippe, Fr. Jacques. *Time for God*. Scepter Publishers, 2008.

[73] St. Josemaria Escriva, *The Way*, Chapter 3, Number 91.

[74] Tucciarone, Tracy. "Lectio Divina," Fish Eaters. <http://www.fisheaters.com/lectiodivina.html> Accessed 9 May 2012.

[75] Socias, Fr. James, ed. *Handbook of Prayers*. Midwest Theological Forum, Woodridge, Ill., 2007.

[76] "A Detailed Catholic Examination of Conscience," Beginning Catholic, <http://www.beginningcatholic.com/catholic-examination-of-conscience.html> Accessed 9 May 2012.

[77] St. Josemaria Escriva, *The Way of the Cross*, 7th station, Point for Meditation #3. Scepter Publishers, Princeton, N.J., 1976.

[78] "Eucharistic Adoration," Catholic Center at UGA, <http://cc.uga.edu/liturgy/adoration.htm> Accessed 9 May 2012.

[79] Lacey, Charles V. *Rosary Novenas to Our Lady*. Benziger Brothers, Woodland Hills, Calif., 1954.

[80] Novena to the Holy Spirit for the Seven Gifts, EWTN.com,

<http://www.ewtn.com/devotionals/pentecost/seven.htm> Accessed 21 May 2012.

[81] Tucciarone, Tracy. "Devotion to the Sacred Heart of Jesus." Fish Eaters. <http://www.fisheaters.com/sh.html> Accessed 9 May 2012.

[82] Tucciarone, Tracy. "Devotion to the Immaculate Heart of Mary." Fish Eaters. <http://www.fisheaters.com/ih.html> Accessed 9 May 2012.

[83] "The Holy Face of Jesus." Our Lady of the Rosary Library. <http://www.olrl.org/pray/holy_face.shtml> Accessed 9 May 2012.

[84] "History of the Message and Devotion to Divine Mercy," The Divine Mercy. Marians of the Immaculate Conception. < http://thedivinemercy.org/message/history/> Accessed 17 May 2012.

[85] "The Chaplet of St. Michael the Archangel." EWTN. <http://www.ewtn.com/devotionals/prayers/chaplet-of-st-michael.htm> Accessed 9 May 2012.

[86] Kellmeyer, Steve, Ibid.

[87] Tucciarone, Tracy. "Introduction to Sacramentals." Fish Eaters. <http://www.fisheaters.com/sacramentalsintro.html> Accessed 9 May 2012.

[88] Hardon, Fr. John. *Modern Catholic Dictionary*. 1980.

[89] Hampsch, Fr. John H. "Blessed Salt." Claretian Teaching Ministry. <http://claretiantapeministry.org/page.asp?t=Blessed%20Salt> Accessed 9 May 2012.

[90] Tucciarone, Tracy. "Fire." Fish Eaters. <http://www.fisheaters.com/fire.html> Accessed 9 May 2012.

[91] Saunder, Fr. William. "Physical Reminders of Our Faith," *The Arlington Catholic Herald*, 6 June 1996.

<http://www.ewtn.com/library/ANSWERS/PHREMIND. htm> Accessed 9 May 2012.

92 Tucciarone, Tracy. "Scapulars." Fish Eaters. <http://www.fisheaters.com/scapulars.html> Accessed 9 May 2012.

93 "The Jubilee Medal of St. Benedict." Our Lady of the Rosary Library. <http://www.olrl.org/sacramental/benedictmedal.shtml > Accessed 9 May 2012.

ABOUT THE AUTHOR

Fr. Richard M. Heilman is a priest for the Diocese of Madison and is pastor of three parishes: St. Ignatius in Mt. Horeb, St. Mary of Pine Bluff, and Holy Redeemer in Perry.

He is the founder of the Knights of Divine Mercy, which is an apostolate for Catholic men's faith formation, and he is a Fourth Degree chaplain for the Knights of Columbus, chaplain for the Madison area Holy Family Homeschoolers, advisory board member of St. Ambrose Academy, and board member of the Women's Care Center.

With his expertise in spiritual direction, Father Heilman is also a regular guest priest on Relevant Radio's, *The Inner Life.*

Father Heilman has a passion for the pro-life cause and is also the founder of Kneel for Life, which encourages all to draw upon God's supernatural strength and power through prayer before all pro-life efforts.

Visit the Knights of Divine Mercy website at www.knightsofdivinemercy.com.

CPSIA information can be obtained at www.ICGtesting.com
Printed in the USA
LVOW10s0003110314

376859LV00012B/155/P